A Hundred Red ROSES

A Cookbook for the New Bride

Satya Sudhir

INDIA • SINGAPORE • MALAYSIA

Notion Press

Old No. 38, New No. 6
McNichols Road, Chetpet
Chennai - 600 031

First Published by Notion Press 2018
Copyright © Satya Sudhir 2018
All Rights Reserved.

ISBN 978-93-86295-88-0

This book has been published with all efforts taken to make the material error-free after the consent of the author. However, the author and the publisher do not assume and hereby disclaim any liability to any party for any loss, damage, or disruption caused by errors or omissions, whether such errors or omissions result from negligence, accident, or any other cause.

No part of this book may be used, reproduced in any manner whatsoever without written permission from the author, except in the case of brief quotations embodied in critical articles and reviews.

Blessed by: Dr. (Mrs.) Sarojini and Mr. John S. Pancharatnam

Released by: Mrs. Susila and Dr. James R. Daniel

First copy gifted to: Mrs. Jasmine and Mr. Jacob R. Daniel

To God be the Glory

"…. A woman that feareth the Lord, she shall be praised"

Proverbs 31:30

Contents

Acknowledgements		viii
A Hundred Red Roses, from Me to You... With Love!		ix
Why Did I Title this Book, 'A Hundred Red Roses'?		xiii

I. **Christmas** ... 1
   1. Chicken Biryani with Pachadi and Boiled Eggs ... 2
   2. Brinjal Curry ... 6
   3. Tomato Jam ... 7
   4. Vermicelli Payasam ... 8
   5. Jaangari ... 10
   6. Boondi & Ladoo ... 11
   7. Badushah ... 12
   8. Adirasam ... 14
   9. Muruku ... 15
   10. Yule Log ... 16

II. **Easter** ... 19
   11. Bread Rolls with Fish Cutlet ... 20
   12. Carrot Cake ... 23
   13. Easter Marble Cake ... 24
   14. Idiyappam and Fish Curry ... 25
   15. Carrot Halwa ... 28
   16. Easter Bunny Carrot Cookies ... 29
   17. Easter Eggs & Chocolates ... 30
   18. Hot Cross Buns and Fish Fry ... 32
   19. Rose Cookies ... 34
   20. Fruit Salad & Custard ... 35

III. **Breakfast** ... 37
   21. Appam & Chicken Curry ... 38
   22. Poori And Potato Curry ... 40
   23. Rava upma and Kesari ... 42
   24. Adai ... 45
   25. Rava Dosai ... 46
   26. Bombay Toast – Sweet and Karam ... 47
   27. Idly, Dosai & Coconut Chutney ... 50
   28. Puttu ... 52
   29. Pancake ... 54
   30. Pongal – Sweet and Ven ... 55

IV. **Lunch Box** ... 58
   31. Chapati and Potato Poriyal ... 59
   32. Chicken Katti Roll ... 61
   33. Coconut Rice and Valaka Fry ... 63
   34. Lemon Rice and Chicken Masala ... 65
   35. Sambar Rice and Chicken Pakoda ... 67
   36. Pepper Rice and Mutton Masala ... 70
   37. Mango Rice and Prawn Fry ... 72
   38. Peas & Soya Pulao ... 74
   39. Spinach Pulao and Chicken Nuggets ... 75
   40. Fried Rice and Gobi Manchurian ... 77

V. Sunday Special – Tea Time Snacks and Treats — 81
41. Bread Bajji — 87
42. Oma Podi — 88
43. Diamond Cuts – Sweet and Karam — 89
44. Doughnuts — 91
45. Samosa — 92
46. Chicken Croquettes — 96
47. Spring Roll — 97
48. Patties — 100
49. Masala Vadai — 103
50. Raised Doughnuts — 104

VI. Everyday Curries — 107
51. Dhal — 112
52. Sambar — 113
53. Puli Kozhambu — 115
54. Channa Kozhambu — 116
55. Keerai Kozhambu — 118
56. Poondu Kozhambu — 120
57. Rasam — 121
58. Pasi Parupu Kozhambu — 122
59. Vendaka Kara Kozhambu — 124
60. Muttai Kozhambu — 126

VII. Everyday Poriyals — 128
61. Carrot and Corn Poriyal — 129
62. Cabbage and Peas Poriyal — 130
63. Cauliflower Fry — 131
64. Potato Fry — 132
65. Beetroot Poriyal — 134
66. Kovakai Poriyal — 135
67. Akuri — 136
68. Avial — 138
69. Cucumber Poriyal — 139
70. Beans Poriyal — 140

VIII. Hobby Time – Baking — 142
71. Brownies — 152
72. Banana Carrot Cake — 153
73. Pineapple upside Down Cake — 154
74. Apple Sponge — 156
75. Date Cake — 158
76. Chocolate Cake — 159
77. Dark Chocolate Biscuit Cheesecake — 160
78. Coffee Cup Cakes — 162
79. Chocolate Chip Cookies — 164
80. Apple Cinnamon Roses — 165

IX. Summer Holidays — 169
81. Mango Kulfi — 173
82. Hot and Sweet Mango Pickle — 174
83. Fish Pickle — 176
84. Mango Juice — 177
85. Raw Mango Juice — 178
86. Lime Juice — 180
87. Hot and Sweet Lime Pickle — 181
88. Chocolate Ice Cream — 182
89. Mango Cake — 183
90. Strawberry Jam & Tri-Colour Sandwich — 184

X. Makeovers with Leftovers — 187
91. Banana Cake — 188
92. Bread Pudding — 189
93. Kothu Parotta — 190
94. Aloo Paratta — 191
95. Pizza — 192
96. Bread Gulab Jamun — 194
97. Rasogollas — 195
98. Banana Paniyaram — 196
99. Rice Kheer — 197
100. Ghee — 198

Appendix — *199*

Acknowledgements

I believe in God. I believe in family. I believe in love.

I dedicate this cookbook to three remarkable God-fearing women in my life who taught me all that I know today about cooking. They are my mothers – Dr. Sarojini Pancharatnam, Mrs. Susila James and my sister – Mrs. Chitra Niranjan

I would like to thank my dad – Mr. J.S Pancharatnam who is the most intelligent, selfless, caring and the greatest man I have ever known in my life. My heartfelt gratitude is also due to Dr. James Reynold Daniel who I affectionately call, *'Papa'* for his encouraging words and support to me always. I would also like to thank my brother-in-law – Mr. Niranjan Nirmalkumar for always being there for me through thick and thin. My gratitude is also due to my dear brother and childhood playmate – Dr. Divyan Pancharatnam, Dr. Maria Sajini, Dr. Sujit Ralin Daniel, Dr. Priscilla Ralin, Dr. Suganth Ryleson Daniel and my dearest handsome nephews – Ethan, Adrien, Akshay and Arvind.

Sudhir and Raynah, all that I am is because of you. Love you so much!

A Hundred Red Roses, from Me to You... With Love!

"Every wise woman buildeth her house...."

Proverbs 14:1

Dear Bride, who thought that I would ever write a cookbook? For that matter, who thought that I would ever learn to cook? Looking back, I realize that my culinary journey has been a very interesting one. With the joys of being newly married in 2009, came responsibilities for both my husband and me. I had to run the home and he had to provide the means to do so. In my case, not only did I not know a thing or two about cooking, but I also discovered in quick course of time that I lacked any sort of aptitude for culinary skills.

For many, cooking sounds like the simplest of household chores. But, believe me, it wasn't for a novice homemaker like me who did not even know how to switch on the gas stove!!! Most mornings were spent browsing Internet sites to find a recipe, decipher it, sort out and acquire the needed ingredients and then finally...cook the dish. There were endless frantic SOS phone calls to my mother, sister and my husband's mother to salvage a dish that was either over-cooked, burnt, over-salted, over-seasoned or was tasteless and flavour-less. That first year of my marriage can be rightly called, 'The year of kitchen goof-ups'. There were daily lessons in geography as chapatis rolled out were far from a round shape but rather resembled a different shapeless country on the map every time. I learnt through a disastrous breakfast attempt that dosai batter had to be fermented the night before before pouring out a dosai the next morning. Potato fries were burnt on the outside and raw on the inside by overheating the oil for frying. I could not even tell the difference between *Rice flour* and *Refined flour* and there were hence disastrous dishes. Oh! (sigh!)...the list of bloopers is endless! Even today I wonder, if during those first few months my just married husband feared what inedible disaster he would have to politely and silently swallow every night at dinner, not wanting to offend his newly wed wife! Hats off to him for being the ever-encouraging spouse by not grumbling. In fact, on days when dishes were far from edible, he even offered to cook instant noodles for me.

My message to you is that it took the love for a man (who loved to eat good food), to turn a kitchen hater like me into a confident cook. With a prayer, I decided to learn to cook. Learning to cook was like learning to read, write and speak a new language where you have to battle with grammar, punctuation, pronunciation and spelling. Some people are blessed and have it in them. They are the born cooks. Others do not have it in them, but take heart, as cooking is a skill that can be acquired and mastered over time through experience and perseverance. Master this language and you will be able to write poetry and songs through your dishes. Sometimes the right attitude overtakes aptitude to be a good cook. I have learnt that it takes a lot of patience to be a good cook. Onions have to be sautéed to transparency for the right flavor, eggs have to be beaten well to get a fluffy omelet and fresh cream has to whisked until soft peaks rise to get the right texture in a pudding. There are also golden rules of thumb for baking and cooking. Remember that nursery rhyme we learnt in kindergarten? "*Some like it hot*" – Ingredients must be warm, at room temperature for cakes and breads... "*Some like it cold*" – Ingredients must be ice cold for cookies and biscuits... "*Some like it in the pot, nine days old*" – An earthen pot is the best for fish curry and it always tastes better on the next day.

To make my endeavour more interesting, I started my very own handwritten personalized recipe book with recipes gathered from all sources. This was so at least I could refer to a set of procedures in steps of 1, 2, & 3 and present something palatable on the dining table. I started off experimenting at first with very small stuff like learning to boil an egg to perfection, boiling milk without it spilling over etc., I also added to my collection a whole range of fancy kitchen gadgets to remove the dull humdrum associated with everyday cooking. The favourites in my kitchen today are a recipe book holder (very useful), kitchen timer (for those absent minded days), measuring cups and spoons (must-haves), kitchen scale (very good for a beginner), assorted cookie cutters, colourful tea towels, oven mitts etc., Thanks to all this, I am now able to cook with confidence, entertain regularly and above all be inspired to enjoy a mundane, day-in-and-day-out task like cooking. By now most of the regular recipes I know by heart but I still collect and write recipes down. I hope someday I will be able to pass on my recipe books to my daughter and granddaughter as 'Grandma's Cook Books'!! (Smile!)

There is no end to what you can learn in cooking and you can never have learnt it all. There is always a new ingredient, a new recipe and a new dish to be tried out and learnt. But above all, the most important ingredient to a dish is love. You need to be in love or love those you are cooking for. Every wife has experienced this. The day you fight with your family, the dish is a disaster! I also feel that cooking is therapeutic and helps you to love those you are cooking for. In my experience, you can never cook and serve a meal to an adversary. I also advocate a personalized recipe collection. Be it in a notebook or a diary, write down the recipe with tips every time it turns out fine and constantly update dos and don'ts. Seeking advice from aunts, grandmas, moms and best friends is the best way to learn the secrets of home cooking. They are also perhaps the best teachers for hand-me-down recipes passed on as family secrets from one generation to the other. There are many other ways also to learn like watching cooking demos on the T.V, the Internet and there are cookbooks galore. And, of course there's no greater motivation than a word of appreciation from your family members, husband and kids.

Since I have scripted this cookbook exclusively for you, there are 100 very basic recipes and tips for everyday cooking as well as entertaining, for your husband's lunch box and for festivals like Christmas & Easter. A separate section has been added exclusively for kids as 'Sunday tea time snacks and treats', which can be used for birthday parties, church picnics and harvest festivals. A hobby section has been added for those who wish to take up baking during weekends. The book ends with a special section on make over recipes using leftovers! At the end of each recipe is a cooking tip, which I hope will be very useful for you as a beginner bride in the kitchen. All the recipes in this book are shared with love from my kitchen to yours. Try them all out as they have been tested and tried many times by me until almost near perfection. Improvise on them and try out your own variations of the recipes. As a new bride, enjoy cooking and entertaining with a smile. But above all else, I advocate prayer. Pray before you plan the day's menu. Ask the Lord to grant you wisdom to run your home in a way that pleases Him. Seek to do the will of God in every chore. Ask the Lord to bless the food that you cook and your family for whom you cook. At the dining table, eat as a family and say grace before partaking of the meal. The results are rewarding.

Why Did I Title this Book, 'A Hundred Red Roses'?

Despite their short vase life, roses have been regarded as symbols of longetivity and love and are the favourite choice for bouquets. As for me, I love the colour and fragrance of roses...there's really nothing quite more beautiful than a table setting with long stemmed roses arranged gracefully in a glass vase as the centrepiece. The rose motif is also my favourite of all designs. Hence in my home, more than often I choose a "roses" theme for special occasions like an anniversary, for Valentine's Day or even evening tea with my mom.

Rose motifs on kitchenware comes in all colour shades like crimson, burgundy, pastel pink, baby blush, summer yellow, lavender and so on. Designs vary from simple abstract to delicate to elaborately decorative. In the kitchen, the rose motif finds its way rather easily on embossed cutlery, prints on crockery, kitchen linen like tablecloths, tea towels, aprons and curtains, cake and chocolate moulds, cookie cutters etc.,

Dear new bride, I titled this recipe collection of mine, 'A hundred red roses' like a gift bouquet of hundred red roses from me, just for you with the hope that you too find everlasting love and happiness in your home, family and kitchen!

Wishing you many happier hours of cooking!

Satya Sudhir

Christmas

"For unto you is born this day in the city of David a Saviour, which is Christ the Lord"

(Luke 2:11)

Christmas is always a special time for everybody especially the new bride. It is the first festival that you celebrate as the "Mrs." with your husband. Everything's new in the first Christmas and yet the festival is so age old. It truly is the most wonderful time of the year. My first Christmas as a new bride was a very special one. But, for that matter haven't all of my Christmas'?

Christmas is a reminder year after year that my Saviour Lord Jesus came down to earth from heaven in all simplicity for my redemption. To celebrate this gift of salvation, I celebrate Christmas in all grandeur with family, friends and festivities. I have wonderful memories of the yuletide season as a child. In my parent's home, Christmas would begin in the first week of December after the first Sunday called the 'Advent'. As we decorated the Christmas tree, with carols playing in the background on my dad's two-in-one, my mother would pass around all sorts of treats. Then, a fortnight before Christmas, large-scale preparation of sweets and savouries for distribution, would begin in the backyard on wooden stoves. A specially engaged cook would be called in to prepare all sorts of delicacies. As kids we would hover around him until to our delight, he would hand us a fresh hot *Jaangari* or *Laddo*, not to mention filling our pockets with sugared *Boondi!* The sweets would then be packed in large ever-silver tins with strict instructions to us kids – "Not to be opened until Christmas". So many precious memories! I dedicate this section to my dad who made every Christmas and my childhood so memorable.

Today, a typical Christmas day in my family begins with *Appam* and *Chicken stew* for breakfast after which the entire family sets off for church service. By noon, cousins, aunts and uncles gather at the ancestral home of grandparents for a sumptuous Christmas lunch of *Chicken biryani* and *Payasam*. Then there are countless rounds of *Adirasams, Mundiri Kothus* and *Murukus* passed around. Rounds of laughter and exchange of gifts wondrously aid in digestion. The evening is always out door either at the beach or around a campfire, singing Christmas carols by candlelight with a supper of barbequed *Kababs,* warm *Bread* and *Chicken curry,* nicely finished off with slices of the traditional *Chocolate yule log* and *Ice cream.*

1. Chicken Biryani with Pachadi and Boiled Eggs

Biryani is truly the king of all dishes. It was the royal dish of kings and princes and today is one of the must-be-served dishes at Indian weddings, functions, special ocassions, office treats etc., And, so I call Biryani a 'Celebration of life' dish.

There are more than a dozen types of biryanis in India. They are all closely related cousins with the main ingredients being the same namely – rice, meat and spices. But each is significantly unique in the method of preparation, taste and appearance. They are the Hyderbadi mutton biryani, the Chettinad nattu kozhi biryani, the Ambur dum biryani, Navratan biryani (with fruits), Tehari or vegetable biryani, Malabar beef biryani, Dindugal thalapa kattu biryani, Fish and prawn biryani, Egg biryani, Dakhni, Rowther, Mughlai, Takari biryani etc.,

Although biryani is a stand-alone dish that can be eaten alone, the taste and biryani eating experience can be further enhanced with a side dish like chicken curry or brinjal curry, boiled eggs, papad or potato chips and a curd salad called Raita or Pachadi. Eating on a banana leaf is for me the right way to eat biryani. There is unexplainable magic in that!

Biryani can become a bachelor's dish in the sense that all it requires is a single pressure cooker or a single pot to cook it. A little chopping, mixing and seasoning... and the dish is ready to be served and eaten and there is just a single dish to wash up. Highly aromatic, spicy and doubly loaded with calories, biryani should be always nicely finished off with a sweet payasam or kheer.

Notes:

1. Though Biryani is quintessentially made with Basmati rice, Seeraga Samba rice can be used to make Chettinad biryani.
2. Meat on bone rather than plain boneless meat adds better flavor to the biryani.

3. The raw smell of meat can be completely removed by washing it in curd before cooking.
4. Chicken does not need pre-cooking but mutton and beef must be pre-cooked separately before adding to the rice.
5. Biryani and *Pulao* use almost the same ingredients and method of preparation, but there are a few differences between the two. *Biryani* is darker in colour and ingredients such as red chily powder and tomatoes are used, whereas *Pulao* is lighter and ingredients such as green chillies, turmeric powder (optional) and coconut milk are used.

Chicken Biryani

Ingredients:

½ kg	–	Chicken with bone
2 cups	–	Basmati Rice (*Basmati arisi*)
3	–	Onions (*Vengayam*), julienned
2	–	Tomatoes (*Thakali*), julienned
2	–	Bay leaf (*Brinji elai*)
1" piece	–	Cinnamon stick (*Pattai*)
5	–	Cloves (*Krambu*)
1 cup	–	Fresh curds (*Thayir*)
2 tsp.	–	Red chili powder (*Milagai podi*)
3 tsp.	–	Coriander powder (*Malli podi*)
2 tbsp.	–	Ginger garlic paste (*Inji poondu viluthu*)

1 bunch	–	Mint leaves (*Pudina elai*), finely chopped
1 bunch	–	Coriander leaves (*Kothamali elai*), finely chopped
3	–	Green chillies (*Pachai milagai*), full; do not chop
1	–	Lime, juice (*Elumichai saaru*)
3 tbsp.	–	Gingelly oil (*Nalla ennai*)
2 tbps	–	Ghee (*Nei*)
½ cup	–	Curds (*Thayir*), for marinating
To taste	–	Salt (*Uppu*)

Method:

1. Wash the chicken under running water 3 times to clean it well and remove all the blood.
2. Marinate the chicken with ½ a cup of curd for half an hour. This will not only remove any unpleasant odour from the chicken but will also soften it
3. Grease the sides of a pressure cooker with ghee. This will prevent the biryani from becoming sticky.
4. Heat 3 tbsp. of oil and 2 tbsp. of ghee in the pressure cooker
5. Add the spices – bay leaves, cinnamon and cloves
6. Add onions and sauté till they slightly brown
7. Add the green chilies
8. Add ginger garlic paste and mix well.
9. Add the chicken
10. Add coriander leaves and mint leaves finely chopped
11. Add tomatoes
12. Add red chili powder and coriander powder and mix well. (Or else use 3 tbsp. of Biryani Masala)
13. Add 3 cups of water and 1 cup of curd.
14. The ratio is 1 cup of rice: 2 cups of (water + curd)
15. Mix well and let the water boil
16. Just before closing the cooker, add limejuice. DO NOT stir or mix after this stage. Close the cooker and let it cook for 3 whistles. The limejuice will also prevent the rice from becoming sticky.

17. Serve piping hot on a banana leaf with onion pachadi, brinjal curry, tomato jam, potato chips and boiled eggs

Tip: For making biryani and pulao, use chicken pieces with bone as they enhance the taste. Boneless chicken pieces can be used to make chicken gravy or chicken mince

Pachadi

Ingredients:

1 cup	–	Fresh curds (*Thayir*)
1	–	Large onion (*Vengayam*), julienned
3	–	Green chillies (*Pachai milagai*), finely chopped
½ cup	–	Coriander leaves (*Kothamali elai*) finely chopped
To taste	–	Salt (*Uppu*)

Method:

Mix all the ingredients well in a bowl
Add salt just before serving

Boiled Eggs

Ingredients:

4	–	Eggs (*Muttai*)
2 tbsp.	–	Salt (*Uppu*)

Method:

1. Heat 3 cups of water in a sauce pan. Add salt to it
2. Drop in the eggs gently, one by one into the salt water
3. When the water boils, turn down the heat to simmer and cook for 30 minutes
4. Remove from heat, cover and let it cool down for 20 minutes
5. De-shell the eggs when completely cool

Note: Adding salt or vinegar to the water in which the eggs are boiled will prevent egg white from oozing out. Also, if cold eggs taken straight from the refrigerator are brought to room temperature before boiling, they will not crack while boiling.

2. Brinjal Curry

In most parts of South India, Biryani is served with 'Salna', which is a gravy of chicken or mutton. But this hot and tangy brinjal curry brings out the flavour of biryani in ways words cannot express. The curry can also be eaten with steamed rice and papad.

Ingredients:

4	–	Brinjals (*Katharikai*), quartered
1 tsp.	–	Mustard (*Kadugu*)
1 tsp.	–	Cumin seeds (*Seeragam*)
1 tsp. + 1 tsp.	–	Peppercorns (*Milagu*)
1 tsp.	–	Fenugreek seeds (*Vendayam*)
3	–	Onions (*Vengayam*), paste
5	–	Tomatoes (*Thakali*), pureed
6 pods	–	Garlic (*Poondu*), crushed
1 tsp.	–	Turmeric powder (*Manjal podi*)
1 tbsp.	–	Coriander powder (*Malli podi*)
1 tbsp.	–	Red chili powder (*Milagai podi*)
1 lime size ball	–	Tamarind, extract (*Puli saaru*)
2 sprigs	–	Curry leaves (*Karuvapaellai*)
4 tbsp.	–	Gingelly oil (*Nalla ennai*)
2 cups	–	Refined sunflower oil for frying (*Poripathuku ennai*)
To taste	–	Salt (*Uppu*)

Method:
1. Heat oil for frying. Lightly fry the brinjal quarters in the hot oil. Remove and keep aside
2. Dry roast 1 tsp. fenugreek, 1 tsp. cumin seeds and 1 tsp. pepper corns
3. Cool and grind to a powder without water
4. In a wok (*kadai*), heat oil
5. Season with mustard and 1 tsp. pepper corns
6. Add curry leaves
7. Add the crushed garlic
8. Add the onion paste
9. Add the fried brinjal pieces and mix well
10. Add the ground powder
11. Add turmeric powder, coriander powder and red chili powder
12. Add tomato puree and salt
13. Cover and cook on simmer till the oil separates and the brinjals soften
14. Add the tamarind extract and bring to a boil

Tip: After cutting the brinjals, soaking them in a bowl of water will prevent blackening.

3. Tomato Jam

Yes indeed, this jam is served with Biryani in sweet contrast to its hot and spicy flavours. The secret to a good tomato jam is in its sweetness and redness. Hence I would advise you to use ripe tomatoes for the preparation. Removing the seeds is matter of a personal choice. The shelf life of this jam is not more than two days as no preservative has been added. But as this jam is so tasty, I doubt it will last more than one meal on the table!

Ingredients:
½ kg	–	Ripe red tomatoes (*Thakali*)
1 kg	–	Sugar (*Sarkarai*)
1	–	Lime, juice (*Elumichai saaru*)

Method:
1. Blanch the tomatoes by dipping them in boiling hot water for a few minutes and then plunging them into cold water. Now the skin will peel off easily. De-skin and keep aside
2. In a large wok (*kadai*), cook the tomatoes along with sugar on simmer
3. When the pulp thickens, add lemon juice
4. Cool and serve with hot biryani

Tip: The same recipe can be used to make pineapple, strawberry and papaya jam. Permitted artificial food colours and essence can also be added if you like.

4. Vermicelli Payasam

A payasam is the South Indian dessert after Biryani. With essential ingredients that aid in digestion, it is the most wonderful way of finishing a festive meal. Payasam is a must serve dish along with vadai during important occasions like house warming events or naming ceremonies.

Ingredients:

½ cup	–	Vermicelli (*Semiya*)
¼ cup	–	Sago (*Javvarisi*)
2 cups	–	Boiled milk (*Kothikavaitha Paal*)
½ cup	–	Condensed milk (*Sundiya Paal*)
1 tbsp.	–	Cardamom powder (*Elakai podi*) for flavor
A pinch	–	Kesari powder (*Kesari podi*) for colour
3 tbsp.	–	Ghee (*Nei*)
¼ cup	–	Raisins (*Ularnta thirachai*)
¼ cup	–	Cashewnuts (*Mundiri*), chopped

Method:

1. In a large sauce pan, heat 2 tbsp. of ghee
2. Add sago and vermicelli. Roast for 1 minute on simmer
3. Add boiled milk
4. Let it cook. When the sago has become transparent and glassy it means it has cooked well
5. Add condensed milk, stirring continuously. Or else add sugar to taste
6. When the payasam thickens, add cardamom powder
7. Add kesari powder and remove from the stove
8. Heat 1tbsp. of ghee in a small seasoning pan (*thalipu karandi*)
9. Fry cashewnuts and raisins
10. Add this to the payasam. Mix well and serve hot

Tip: The quantity of vermicelli may seem insufficient in the recipe but do not be tempted to add more. Even a little vermicelli swells up in volume when cooked and is more than sufficient. Adding too much will thicken the payasam and will not taste good.

5. Jaangari

This is a popular sweet that is served at all South Indian weddings and festivals but it can also be found sold on the street as street food! Making this sweet requires immense skill and practise, as the batter must be piped swiftly into flowerly swirls, directly into hot oil. Once fried, the jaangari is drained off its oil and put into a pre-prepared sugar syrup where it swells in size after soaking up all the sugar. Sugar acts as a sweetener as well as a preservative here.

Ingredients:

1 cup	–	Black gram (*Ullutham parupu*)
1 tbsp	–	Rice flour (*Arasi mavu*)
2 cups	–	Sugar (*Sarkarai*)
½ cup approx	–	Water
1 tbsp.	–	Rose essence (*Roja saarai*)
¼ tsp. + ¼ tsp.	–	Orange colour
3 cups	–	Refined sunflower oil for frying (*Poripathuku ennai*)

Method:

1. Take sugar in a thick bottom wok (*kadai*). Add water just enough to cover the sugar. Heat until the sugar dissolves, stirring constantly
2. Add rose essence and ¼ tsp. orange colour
3. Keep heating until ½ string consistency is reached. The sugar syrup is ready
4. Soak together urad dhal overnight
5. Grind well to get a very smooth but thick batter
6. Add the rice flour and ¼ tsp. orange colour. Mix well

7. Put the batter in a piping bag
8. Heat oil for frying and pipe flower shaped jaangaris directly into the hot oil. Let it cook for 5 minutes
9. Remove from heat and directly soak in sugar syrup for a few minutes. Remove and keep aside.

Tip: The North Indian cousin of Jaangari is '*Jalebi*' which is made from flour instead of black gram. The method of preparation is the same. Jalebi is served with milk both at breakfast as well as a snack before dinner.

6. Boondi & Ladoo

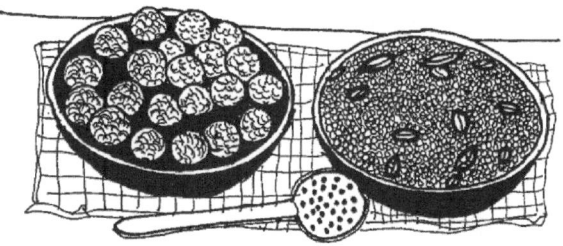

Hoping for two birds with one stone? Then this is the recipe for you. The first step involves making the Boondi, which can be either made into savoury Boondi and mixture by adding salt and other spicy ingredients. Dipping the Boondi in sugar syprup gives you sweet Boondi. Rolling the sweet Boondi into rounds gives you another sweet, the Ladoo.

Ingredients:

1 cup	–	Bengal gram flour (*Kadala mavu*)
1-½ cups	–	Sugar (*Sarkarai*)
¼ tsp.	–	Baking soda (*Aapa soda*)
10	–	Cloves (*Krambu*)
1 tsp.	–	Cardamom powder (*Elakai podi*)
8	–	Cashewnuts (*Mundiri*), quartered
8	–	Raisins (*Ularnta thirachai*)
1 tsp.	–	Ghee (*Nei*)
3 cups	–	Refined sunflower oil for frying (*Poripathuku ennai*)

Method:

1. Mix together Bengal gram flour, baking soda and water to get a batter of flowing liquid consistency
2. Heat oil for frying in a wok (*kadai*)
3. Place a ladle with large holes (*boondi karandi*) over the wok
4. Pour a little batter on the ladle so that it falls into the oil like raindrops
5. Deep fry for a few minutes. Remove and keep aside to drain the oil
6. In a small seasoning pan (*thalipu karandi*) fry cashewnuts and raisins in 1 tsp. ghee. Remove and keep aside
7. In a large thick bottom wok, heat sugar with ½ cup of water until 2 string consistency is reached
8. Remove from heat and keep the sugar syrup aside to cool slightly
9. When it cools, mix together the fried boondi, cashewnuts and raisins in the syrup. Now the boondi is ready!
10. To make ladoos, mix the boondi again. Let it rest for 5 minutes.
11. Mix again. Let it rest for 5 minutes. Repeat this procedure 5 times
12. When the sugar has crystallised, smear a little ghee in your palm. Roll out the boondi and shape them into small balls. The ladoos are ready.

Tip: Repeated mixing and resting the boondi is very essential to get a uniform coating of sugar on each and every boondi. For a different flavor, optionally you can add a clove or kalkandu to each ladoo while rolling up the boondi

7. Badushah

This sweet is a like a fried pastry of South India and its richness depends on the soft, flaky texture of the crust. Though it is packed with calories, it is mild in sweetness compared to other sweets

Ingredients:

1 cup	–	Flour (*Maida mavu*)
3 tbsp.	–	Ghee (*Nei*)
¼ tsp.	–	Baking powder
¼ tsp.	–	Baking soda (*Aapa soda*)
1 tsp.	–	Cardamom powder (*Elakai podi*)
1 tsp.	–	Sugar (*Sarkarai*), for grinding the cardamom
3 cups	–	Refined sunflower oil for frying (*Poripathuku ennai*)

Syrup:

1 cup	–	Sugar
½ cup	–	Water

Method:

1. Mix together ghee, baking powder, baking soda and cardamom powder to make a paste
2. Add this paste to the flour and mix well
3. Sprinkle water (do not pour!) and knead into a soft dough
4. Make medium size smooth balls
5. Flatten out lightly and make a depression in the centre using your thumb
6. Deep fry in medium hot oil so that the badushah cooks fully
7. Meanwhile, prepare the sugar syrup by boiling water and sugar together
8. When 1 string consistency is reached, remove the sugar syrup from the fire
9. Dip the fried badushah in this sugar syrup till it is fully coated with sugar on all sides

Tip: Powdered cardamom can be prepared by grinding it with sugar. Adding powdered cardamom to a sweet dish is better than adding cardamom as a whole.

8. Adirasam

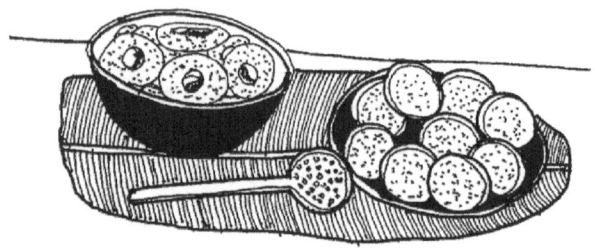

This traditional sweet is like the doughnut of South India. Made with rice and jaggery as the main ingredients the dough is shaped into rounds. These are flattened in the greased palm of the hand and then deep-fried in ho oil. Making the dough must be done at the right time and needs a little muscle power but once it is made, it can be refrigerated and adirasams can be made at any time as required. Jaggery is the sweetener in this sweet. During South Indian weddings, at the send off ceremony of the bride, large tins of muruku and adirasam are sent to the groom's home.

Ingredients:

2 cups	–	Raw rice (*Pacha Arasi*)
2 grains	–	Fennel seeds (*Sombu*)
2 tsp.	–	Cardamom powder (*Elakai podi*)
½ tsp.	–	Dry ginger (*Chukku*)
2 cups	–	Jaggery (*Vellam*)
1 cup	–	Water
3 cups	–	Refined sunflower oil for frying (*Poripathuku ennai*)

Method:

1. Soak raw rice for 4 hours
2. Drain the water completely
3. While wet itself, grind to a fine rice powder with fennel seeds, cardamom powder and dry ginger
4. Sift the ground powder to remove lumps and get a fine powder
5. Heat the jaggery with water until the jaggery dissolves
6. Remove from heat and filter the syrup to remove all the dirt and impurities

7. Place the filtered clean syrup back on the stove and re-heat until the right consistency is reached. To check the consistency of the syrup put a small drop into a bowl of water. The drop must form a globule in the water and not dissolve. This soft ball is the right consistency
8. Remove the syrup from heat and add the rice powder. Mix vigorously to get a paste like dough
9. Smear a little ghee in your palms and make lime size balls from the dough
10. Flatten out the balls on a well-greased banana leaf. You can also use a greased plastic sheet or a plate
11. Heat oil for frying. Deep fry the adirasam in oil until dark brown
12. Place the fried adirasam in the adirasam press or sandwich it between two skimmers and press lightly or else drain the to drain out all the oil

Tip: Do not drain all the oil completely from the adirasam and make it dry. Retaining a little oil on the adirasam keeps it moist and soft for many days and also is a taste enhancer

9. Muruku

'*Muruku*' literally means 'twisted' in Tamil. There are more than 50 varieties of muruku, which can be made by either twisting the dough in your hand (*Kai muruku*) or by using a press with different nozzle shapes. Given below is the basic recipe.

Ingredients:

4 cups	–	Rice flour (***Arasi mavu***)
½ cup	–	Bengal gram flour (***Kadala mavu***)

½ cup	–	Roasted bengal gram flour (*Pottu kadala mavu*)
1 tbsp.	–	Cumin seeds (*Seeragam*)
1-½ tbsp.	–	Unsalted butter (*Vennai*)
¼ tsp.	–	Asafoetida (*Perungayam*)
1 tsp.	–	Black sesame seeds (*Karupu ellu*)
To taste	–	Salt (*Uppu*)
3 cups	–	Refined sunflower oil for frying (*Poripathuku ennai*)

Method:
1. Sift together rice flour, Bengal gram flour, Roasted Bengal gram flour and salt
2. Add butter and mix well
3. Sprinkle water gradually and make a soft dough
4. Fill the greased muruku press with the dough. Use a single star plate in the press
5. Squeeze out the muruku directly into hot oil and deep fry

Tip: Take care while adding butter to the dough because butter will make the muruku soft, but adding too much butter will make the muruku too soft and it will crumble in the oil while frying

10. Yule Log

A Chocolate Swiss Roll with a rugged chocolate icing all around that makes it look like a log of wood is the Chocolate log cake. A few Christmas embellishments like cherries and leaves make it the '*Yule Log*'.

Ingredients:

¾ cup	–	Flour (*Maida mavu*)
3	–	Eggs (*Muttai*)
¾ cup	–	Sugar (*Sarkarai*)
1 tsp.	–	Vanilla essence (*Vanilla saarai*)
1 tbsp.	–	Cocoa powder (*Cocoa thul*)
1 tbsp.	–	Warm water

Filling and Icing:

200 g	–	Butter (*Vennai*)
2 cups	–	Icing sugar (*Icing sarkarai*)
1 tbsp.	–	Cocoa powder (*Cocoa thul*)
2 tbsp.	–	Boiled Milk (*Kothikavaitha Paal*)

Decorations for the Yule log:
Plastic green holly leaves and red cherries in bunches

Method:
1. Whisk eggs, sugar and vanilla essence till thick, light and fluffy
2. Sift flour and cocoa together three times. Gently fold the sifted ingredients into the eggs mixture
3. Carefully add warm water
4. Pour out the batter into a grease and lined Swiss roll tray

5. Bake in a preheated oven at 205°C for 10 minutes
6. While hot itself, turn over onto a butter paper sprinkled with Sugar

7. Carefully roll up into a log shape and keep aside to cool in the paper for 5 minutes

8. Meanwhile, prepare the filling and icing by beating together icing sugar and butter with a little milk to get a soft spreading consistency. Divide into 2 parts. Leave one part plain and to one part add cocoa to get chocolate icing.

9. Unroll the cake roll and spread the plain icing inside.

10. Remove the paper and re-roll the cake into a log shape. Spread the chocolate icing all around the roll to fully cover it
11. Using a fork, draw irregular lines on the icing so that the roll resembles a wooden log

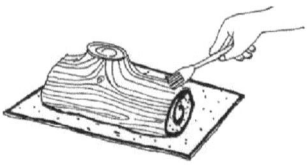

12. Decorate with holly or any other Christmas decorations
13. While serving, cut into slices and serve with ice cream

Tip: Rolling up the cake while hot itself makes it easy to work with and also helps to retain the shape

Easter

"Jesus then cometh, and taketh bread, and giveth them, and fish."

(John 21:13)

Easter is a festival of celebration and new life. The Easter bunny symbolizes this, and is the most commercial representation of Easter along with Easter eggs and carrots. In the Biblical context, after Jesus' resurrection from the dead He appeared to His disciples and ate fish, bread and honey with them. Hence most of the recipes in this section are fish and carrot based. It has been a long-standing tradition to eat hot cross buns on Good Friday after the 3-hour service of remembrance at church, so I have included the recipe here. Though we still continue to celebrate Easter year after year now, my best memories of Easter go back to my childhood when the day before Easter, i.e., on Holy Saturday, the church sextant would bring a kilo of **Seer** fish *(Vanjiram meen)* to the home of each and every member of the women's fellowship. My mom being a part of this wing, would like the other moms, make fish cutlets early in the morning on Easter and we would take them to parish hall in church where they would be gathered from everyone's home. The entire church would be beautifully decorated with white and orange Easter lilies. After the communion service, the entire congregation would have a breakfast fellowship of buns, cutlets and cake.

Back at home, my mom and aunts would prepare a sumptuous Easter lunch of steamed rice and fish curry. It was a welcome non-vegetarian meal after the 40 day long period of lent when we would abstain from eating meat. After that we would head out for egg hunting, i.e a game of treasure hunt for Easter eggs hidden by my uncle in the garden. My cousins and I would most excitedly gather up the eggs in our decorated baskets and feast on the candy inside them, all afternoon. Dessert was either Fruit salad in custard or Carrot halwa with vanilla ice cream. Dinner was usually iddiyappam served with fish curry. The Easter hangover offered tons of innovation to my cousins and me, in our childhood. Leftover rose cookies that were stored in large tins would be smuggled out of the storeroom and coarsely powdered with the '*Ammi*' by the oldest (strongest?) cousin. All the younger cousins would get their carefully proportioned portions in newspaper bundles or handkerchiefs, which we would take away to feast on the terrace. Easter was and is a special time of the year.

11. Bread Rolls with Fish Cutlet

Bread Rolls

Ingredients:

4 cups	–	Flour (*Maida mavu*)
2 tbsp.	–	Fresh yeast (*Pudiya yeast*)
2 tsp.	–	Salt (*Uppu*)
1-½ tbsp.	–	Sugar (*Sarkarai*)
1 cup	–	Warm water
30 g	–	Butter, melted (*Vennai*)

Method:
1. Dissolve yeast in lukewarm water
2. Add salt and sugar. Mix well and keep aside for 10 minutes
3. Add water with yeast and sugar to the flour and knead well
4. Add melted butter and knead again into a soft dough
5. Divide into equal size round balls. Keep aside for 10 minutes
6. Work the balls again and shape them into long rolls
7. Place the rolls on a greased baking tray
8. Keep aside for 45 minutes till they double in size
9. Sprinkle water on them and bake at 200°C for 10 minutes

Fish Cutlet

Ingredients:

2 large slices	–	Seer fish (*Vanjiram meen*)
3	–	Potatoes (*Urulaikkilangu*)
½ tsp.	–	Fennel seeds (*Sombu*)
1	–	Onions (*Vengayam*), finely chopped
5	–	Shallots (*Sambar vengayam*), finely chopped
1	–	Green chilies (*Pachai milagai*), finely chopped
1 tbsp.	–	Ginger garlic paste (*Inji poondu viluthu*)
½ tsp.	–	Turmeric powder (*Manjal podi*)
1 tsp.	–	Coriander powder (*Malli podi*)
1 tsp.	–	Red chili powder (*Milagai podi*)
1 tsp. + ½ tsp.	–	Pepper powder (*Milagu thul*)
1 lime	–	Lime juice (*Elumichai saaru*)
1 sprig	–	Curry leaves (*Karuvapaellai*), finely chopped
½ cup	–	Coriander leaves (*Kothamali elai*), finely chopped
1 egg	–	Egg white (*Muttai venkaru*)
1-½ cups	–	Bread crumbs (*Rotti thul*)
1 tbsp.	–	Gingelly oil (*Nalla ennai*)
3 cups	–	Refined sunflower oil for frying (*Poripathuku ennai*)

Method:

1. Boil the potatoes. Remove the skin and mash them. Keep aside
2. In a wok, cook the fish slices with turmeric powder, salt and a cup of water. Cover and cook under a lid till the fish is cooked and turns white
3. Cool. De-bone the fish patiently
4. In a wok, heat oil
5. Add fennel seeds
6. Add onions and green chilies
7. Add curry leaves
8. Add ginger garlic paste
9. Add coriander powder, red chili powder and salt
10. Add the cooked fish and mix well
11. Add 1 tsp. pepper powder
12. Add coriander leaves
13. Add limejuice. Remove from heat immediately
14. Add mashed potatoes and mix well
15. Shape into cutlets either round, oblong or diamond shape
16. Beat egg white with ½ tsp. pepper powder well
17. Dip each cutlet in egg white
18. Roll in bread crumbs so that it evenly coats the cutlet on all sides
19. Deep fry in hot oil

Tip: To make firm cutlets that will hold their shape and which are not soggy and soft, ensure that there is no moisture in the mashed potatoes or any other ingredient. A little corn flour can be added to the mashed potatoes while mixing. This will hold everything together and you can make firmer cutlets.

12. Carrot Cake

Ingredients:

1 cup	–	Grated carrot (*Thuruviya carrot*)
1-½ cups	–	Flour (*Maida mavu*)
1 cup	–	Sugar (*Sarkarai*)
2	–	Eggs (*Muttai*)
1 tsp.	–	Vanilla essence (*Vanilla saarai*)
¾ cup	–	Refined sunflower oil (*Ennai*)
¾ tsp.	–	Baking soda (*Aapa soda*)
½ tsp.	–	Salt (*Uppu*)
½ tsp.	–	Cinnamon powder (*Ilavankappaṭṭai thuḷ*)
½ tsp.	–	Grated coconut (*Thuruviya thengai*)
½ cup	–	Cashew nuts, chopped (*Mundiri*)

Method:

1. Cream eggs and sugar
2. Add vanilla essence
3. Sift flour, baking powder, salt and cinnamon powder
4. Add to the egg mixture and mix well
5. Add grated coconut
6. Add oil and blend well
7. Pour into a greased and floured cake tin

8. Dust the chopped cashew nuts in Flour and sprinkle on top
9. Bake in a pre-heated oven for 45 minutes at 180°
10. When completely cool, cut into slices and serve with a generous drizzle of chocolate sauce on top

Tip: Cakes must be cooled completely before icing. Never pour icing on a hot cake, as this will melt the icing. For icing designs, mark it first on the cake with a toothpick. Now pipe out the icing on top of the marking.

13. Easter Marble Cake

Ingredients:

1 cup	–	Flour (*Maida mavu*)
150 g	–	Butter (*Vennai*)
1-¼ cups	–	Sugar (*Sarkarai*)
4	–	Eggs (*Muttai*)
2 tbsp.	–	Cocoa powder (*Cocoa thul*)
2 tbsp.	–	Boiled milk (*Kothikavaitha Paal*)
1 tsp.	–	Baking powder
1 tsp.	–	Vanilla essence (*Vanilla saarai*)
¼ tsp. each	–	Colours; pink and green

Method:
1. Cream butter and sugar
2. Separate eggs
3. Stir in well whisked egg yolks and blend well

4. Add vanilla essence and blend again
5. Sift flour and baking powder 3 times
6. Whisk egg whites well. Add spoonfulls of flour, each time beating thoroughly
7. Add the butter cream mixture
8. Separate into 3 equal portions
9. First portion: Add cocoa powder and blend well
10. Second portion: Add pink colour and blend well
11. Third portion: Add green colour and blend well
12. Pour the three portions of batter alternately into a greased and floured cake tin. Swirl the tin slightly so as to get a marble effect in the batter. Do not mix with a spoon!
13. Bake in a preheated oven at 180' for 45 minutes
14. When the cake has cooled, decorate with butter cream icing or chocolate icing and add an easter motif on top

Tip: The same recipe can be used to bake multi-colour cakes and special cakes on Independence Day, by using green and orange food colour. The effect is spectacular. Do note that the colour of the batter is always lighter than the baked cake.

14. Idiyappam and Fish Curry

Idiyappam

Ingredients:

1 cup	–	Rice flour (*Arasi mavu*)
¾ cup approx.	–	Hot water (*Venneer*)
A pinch	–	Salt (*Uppu*)

Method:
1. Boil water with salt
2. Take Rice flour in a deep bowl and make a well
3. Pour boiling water into the well and knead the rice flour well to get a soft dough
4. Put the dough into the idiyappam maker with a fine holes sieve
5. Grease the idiyappam trays with a little ghee
6. Squeeze out the idiyappam onto the tray in concentric circles
7. Boil water in the idiyappam cooker
8. When the water boils, place the trays inside. Cover and steam cook for 7 minutes
9. Serve hot with fish curry

Fish Curry

Ingredients:

1 kg	–	Seer fish (*Vanjiram meen*), approx. 6–7 large pieces
2 large	–	Onions (*Vengayam*), finely chopped
10	–	Shallots (*Sambar vengayam*), finely chopped
4	–	Tomatoes (*Thakali*), pureed
12 pods	–	Garlic (*Poondu*)
3	–	Green chilies (*Pachai milagai*)
½ tsp.	–	Turmeric powder (*Manjal podi*)
2 tbsp.	–	Coriander powder (*Malli podi*)
1 tbsp.	–	Red chili powder (*Milagai podi*)
1 tbsp.	–	Tamarind paste (*Puli saaru*)

1 tsp.	–	Mustard (*Kadugu*)
1 tsp.	–	Fenugreek seeds (*Vendayam*)
1 tbsp.	–	Fennel seeds (*Sombu*), dry roasted and crushed lightly
1 cup	–	Coconut milk (*Thengai paal*)
2 sprigs	–	Curry leaves (*Karuvapaellai*)
6 tbsp.	–	Gingelly oil (*Nalla ennai*)
To taste	–	Rock Salt (*Kal uppu*)
1 cup	–	Limejuice (*Elumichai saaru*) or buttermilk for cleaning the fish

Method:
1. Wash the fish well with limejuice or buttermilk. This will remove all the bad fish odour. Keep aside
2. In a large pot, heat oil
3. Season with mustard and fenugreek seeds
4. Add onions and shallots and sauté well till they turn transparent
5. Add fennel seeds
6. Cut the head and tail portions of green chilies and add the chilies as a whole
7. Add garlic
8. Add 1 sprig of curry leaves
9. Add turmeric powder, coriander powder and red chili powder
10. Add tomato puree and salt
11. When the oil separates, add tamarind paste dissolved in 2 cups of hot water
12. Add the fish pieces. Cover and cook on simmer for 15 minutes till the fish has cooked and has turned white
13. Add coconut milk and let it boil for just 5 minutes
14. Sprinkle 1 sprig of curry leaves on top. Do not stir. Remove from heat
15. Cover and keep aside until serving time

Tip: To avoid watering of the eyes while cutting onions, soak them in cold water for an hour before peeling. Or else refrigerate them for a day before use.

15. Carrot Halwa

Ingredients:

¾ kg	–	Grated carrot (*Thuruviya carrot*)
5 cups	–	Boiled milk (*Kothikavaitha Paal*)
1 cup	–	Condensed milk (*Sundiya Paal*)
¼ cup	–	Sugar (*Sarkarai*)
¼ tsp.	–	Cardamom powder (*Elakai podi*)
4 tbsp.	–	Ghee (*Nei*)
12, halved	–	Cashewnuts (*Mundiri*)

Method:

1. Add grated carrot to milk and bring to a boil
2. Add sugar and mix well
3. Add condensed milk and cook on simmer for 25 minutes
4. Add cardamom powder ground with 1 tsp. sugar
5. When it is almost dry, add ghee and let it cook
6. Add cashewnuts and serve hot

Tip: If the pan in which you are cooking gets burnt, soak it overnight in water with salt added. It will be easy to clean the following morning

16. Easter Bunny Carrot Cookies

Ingredients:

1	–	Carrot, cooked and mashed
2 cups	–	Flour (*Maida mavu*)
1	–	Eggs (*Muttai*)
1-½ cups	–	Sugar (*Sarkarai*)
½ cup	–	Butter (*Vennai*)
1-½ tsp.	–	Baking powder
1 tsp.	–	Vanilla essence (*Vanilla saarai*)
½ tsp.	–	Salt (*Uppu*)
1 tsp.	–	Orange colour

Method:
1. Cook the carrot and mash well. Cool well
2. Whisk butter and sugar
3. Add well beaten egg
4. Add vanilla essence
5. Add carrot mash
6. Sift flour, baking powder and salt 3 times.
7. Add this and make dough. Knead well
8. Roll out on a floured board
9. Using a bunny shaped cookie cutter cut out bunny shaped cookies

10. Place the cookies in a greased and floured cookie tray leaving ample space between the cookies
11. Bake in a preheated oven at 180' for 12–15 minutes
12. Serve with whipped cream or just eat them plain

Tip: Dip the cookie cutter in flour each time before cutting the dough to get clean and neat edges on each cookie

17. Easter Eggs & Chocolates

Easter Eggs

Ingredients:

6 cups	–	Boiled milk (*Kothikavaitha Paal*)
4 cups	–	Sugar (*Sarkarai*)
1 cup	–	Butter (*Vennai*)
2 cups	–	Cashewnuts (*Mundiri*), powdered
1 tsp.	–	Vanilla essence (*Vanilla saarai*)
Few drops	–	Colours: pink and green

Method:

1. Mix together milk, sugar and butter in a pan. Bring to a boil over heat
2. Simmer and stir continuously till the mixture thickens

3. Add cashewnuts and vanilla essence.
4. When it forms a soft ball stage, remove from heat. Cool well
5. Divide into 2 portions. Add pink to one portion and green to the other
6. Knead well and form egg shapes
7. Cut each egg into 2 and core out the inside
8. Fill with insides with gems or chocolates
9. Seal the halves together again with icing
10. Let it dry. Wrap up the eggs in shiny wrapping paper and decorate with ribbons or easter embellishments

Chocolates

Ingredients:

¼ cup	–	Milk powder *(Paal podi)*
¼ cup	–	Cocoa powder *(Cocoa thul)*
75 g	–	Cocoa Butter *(Cocoa vennai)*
1/3 cup	–	Powdered sugar *(Poditha sarkarai)*

Method:

1. In a double boiler, melt cocoa butter
2. Add milk powder and stir it in to avoid lumps
3. Add powdered sugar and mix well
4. Once the sugar melts and is nicely mixed, add cocoa powder
5. Mix well and pour into a greased plate or you can use a chocolate mould
6. Allow to set in the refrigerator
7. Cut into squares when cold

Tip: Never use a metal spoon or scrubber on a non-stick coated pot or pan. Use only plastic scrubbers for washing and wooden spoons for cooking. If the special coating erodes, discard the vessel immediately.

18. Hot Cross Buns and Fish Fry

Hot Cross Buns

Ingredients:

4 cups	–	Flour (*Maida mavu*)
1 tsp., level	–	Salt (*Uppu*)
25 g	–	Butter (*Vennai*)
1 cup	–	Dried fruits, raisins, cherries (*Ularnta pazhangal, thirachai, cherie*)
½ cup	–	Candied peel (*Candie pazhangal*)
1 tsp.	–	Cinnamon and nutmeg powder (*Ilavankappattai thul, Jathikai thul*)
1	–	Eggs (*Muttai*)
1 cup	–	Boiled milk (*Kothikavaitha Paal*) + water
1 tsp.	–	Fresh yeast (*Pudiya yeast*)
1 tbsp.	–	Sugar (*Sarkarai*)
1 tsp.	–	Water for the glaze
1 cup	–	Flour (*Maida mavu*) made into dough with water for marking the crosses

Method:
1. Sift flour and spice powder
2. Put the flour in a kneading plate and make a well in the centre

3. Dissolve the yeast with 1 tsp. sugar in 100 ml of water
4. After 10 minutes, when the bubbles appear, pour into the well
5. Add butter and egg whisked well
6. Knead into a smooth dough
7. Add fruits and knead again. Keep aside till it doubles in size
8. Divide into 12 portions. Form into buns
9. Arrange on a greased and floured tray
10. Make thin strips to form crosses. Dampen and lay on top of the buns
11. Bake at 232' for 15 minutes on the top rack

Fish Fry

Ingredients:

10	–	Small fish for frying
1 tsp.	–	Turmeric powder (*Manjal podi*)
2 tbsp.	–	Red chili powder (*Milagai podi*)
2 tbsp.	–	Coriander powder (*Malli podi*)
1 tsp.	–	Pepper powder (*Milagu thul*)
2 sprigs	–	Curry leaves (*Karuvapaellai*)
3	–	Limes made into juice (*Elumichai saaru*)
To taste	–	Salt (*Uppu*)
1 cup	–	Refined sunflower oil for grilling (*Poripathuku ennai*)

Method:

1. De-scale the fish and clean each fish well with lime juice
2. Make 3–4 slashes on either side of the fish
3. Make a marinade of turmeric powder, coriander powder, red chili powder, pepper powder, lime juice and salt
4. Marinate the fish well with this masala. Let it rest for 15 minutes
5. Heat oil in a grill pan

6. Fry the fish till it darkens and gets cooked. The flesh of the fish will turn white when fully cooked
7. Serve hot with hot cross buns garnished with lime wedges, carrots, cucumber and onion

Tip: Uncooked fish can be stored for several days in the freezer after marinating with salt, turmeric powder and limejuice. Whenever necessary, thaw it completely before cooking either in a curry or a fry. This applies to all types of non-vegetarian meats too.

19. Rose Cookies

Unlike a typical baked cookie, these cookies are made from a batter and deep-fried. A special mould is first dipped in the batter and then in hot oil. The fried cookies resemble a dainty rose flower with petals, hence their name. They are crunchy and crisp but have a fragile texture. While preparing the batter ensure that the batter is of the right consistency. If the batter is too thick, the rose cookies will not be crisp. If the batter is too think, rose cookies will stick to the mould.

Ingredients:

1 cup	–	Flour (*Maida mavu*)
½ cup	–	Rice flour (*Arasi mavu*)
1	–	Eggs (*Muttai*)
1 cup	–	Sugar (*Sarkarai*)
1 cup	–	Coconut milk (*Thengai paal*)
1 tsp.	–	Sesame seeds (*Ellu*)
A pinch	–	Salt (*Uppu*)

| 3 cups | – | Refined sunflower oil for frying |
| | | *(Poripathuku ennai)* |

Method:
1. Mix all the above ingredients to get a runny batter
2. Dip the well-greased cookie ladle in the batter. The ladle should not be fully dipped in the batter but only ¾th. This way the cookie will slip out easily into the oil
3. Dip the ladle in hot oil to release the cookie. You can use a spoon to release the cookie if necessary. Deep fry.

Tip: The cookie ladle should be soaked in oil for two days. Once it is well greased, it can be used. This is very important. At the time of making the rose cookies, soak the ladle in hot oil before dipping in the batter.

20. Fruit Salad & Custard

This dessert is best served chilled. The must be prepared the previous day and left to set in in the refrigerator. The fruits can also be chopped and stored in the refrigerator in a separate bowl. Do not mix the fruits with custard until serving time, as they will lose their crunchiness. Seasonal fruits like ripe mangoes during summer may be used along with custard or else mixed fruits like grapes, oranges, bananas and apples may be used. Remember to de-seed all the fruits.

Ingredients:

| 4 cups | – | Fruits: Apples, seedless Grapes, Papaya, Banana, Oranges, chopped *(Pazhangal)* |
| 2 tbsp. | – | Vanilla flavoured custard powder *(Cuzhl thul)* |

2-½ cups	–	Boiled milk (*Kothikavaitha Paal*)
3 tbsp.	–	Sugar (*Sarkarai*)
¼ cup	–	Condensed milk (*Sundiya Paal*)

Method:

1. Dissolve custard powder in 3 tbsp. cold milk and keep aside
2. Heat the remaining milk and add sugar. Stir continuously to dissolve the sugar and prevent burning
3. Add the custard powder mix slowly to the boiling milk, stirring continuously for 2 minutes
4. Remove from heat and add condensed milk
5. Cool well
6. Refrigerate to set the custard for 2 hours. Do not freeze
7. Place all the cut fruits in a bowl and cover with cling wrap for 2 hours
8. Mix the fruits with the custard and refrigerate again until serving time.

Tip: To prevent a skin forming on the top of custard, sprinkle a little sugar on top. Also, just one seasonal fruit like mango can be used instead of a mixture of many fruits with custard. But never use pineapple or sweet lime in a fruit salad. Also, do not use any other flavor of custard powder for this recipe except Vanilla

Breakfast

"She riseth also while it is yet night, and giveth meat to her household..."

(Proverbs 31:15)

Good morning! Whoever formulated the old adage, *'Breakfast like a king'* definitely knew what he was talking about for there are so many varieties of breakfast that you can not only enjoy eating but also enjoy cooking them every morning.

A typical South Indian vegetarian breakfast consists of *Idly, Vadai* or *Dosai* with *Sambar* and different types of *Chutney*. A finely brewed filter coffee or tea is served piping hot along with this. There are atleast 100 different types of dosais like *Ragi dosai, Set dosai, Ghee paper roast, Neer dosai, Masala dos*ai and so on. *Rava dosai* is one of my favourite vegetarian breakfast recipes. It needs no overnight soaking or grinding, just a little chopping and a good mix of all the ingredients. Left over batter can be refrigerated and used whenever needed. One of the healthiest breakfast recipes is *Adai,* which has actually an overdose of lentils, but so very tasty when made with ghee.

Appam is one of my favourite breakfast dishes and is traditionally served with sweetened coconut milk. It can also be served with mutton stew or chicken curry. "*Muttai Appam*" is made with a bullseye (egg) in the centre and "*Surprise Appam*" has a little meat filling inside. My special breakfast for sudden and unexpected guests in the morning is *Upma* and *Kesari,* which needs no prior preparation, needs no side dish and can be made quickly and easily.

Puttu is the breakfast of the coast. Steam cooked with just rice flour in a special '*Puttu kuzhal*', it is eaten with bananas and sugar. It is also served with *Brown chickpeas curry*. There are many types of puttu. Usually grated coconut is used to separate the piled layers but layers of mixed vegetable masala or minced meat can also be used. Besides rice flour puttu, which is called '*Vellai puttu*', there are other ingredients used to make puttu and are called *Ragi puttu, Corn puttu, Sooji Wheat puttu, Tapioca puttu* etc.

Continental breakfast is primarily flour based and you can make waffles, pancakes, croissants, doughnuts etc., served with orange juice. A simple English breakfast consists of toasted bread with butter, jam, eggs and bacon nicely finished off with tea. I love the crunch of freshly toasted hot bread with jam melting on top. The recipe for **French toast** was imported into India and took the name **Bombay toast!** Good morning indeed!

21. Appam & Chicken Curry

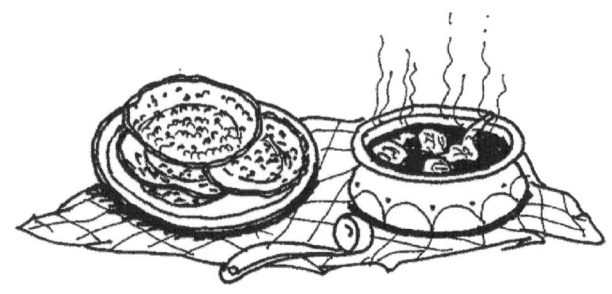

Appam

Ingredients:

1 cup	–	Raw rice (***Pacha Arasi***), uncooked
1 cup	–	Boiled rice (***Pulangal Arasi***), cooked
1 cup	–	Grated coconut (***Thuruviya thengai***)
1 cup	–	Water
½ tbsp.	–	Dry yeast (***Ularnta yeast***)
6 tbsp.	–	Sugar (***Sarkarai***)
A pinch	–	Salt (***Uppu***)

Method:

1. Soak raw rice for 8 hours
2. Mix all the ingredients except salt and grind well in the mixer until the batter starts bubbling and you get the aroma of Appam. The texture of the batter should be silky smooth and not grainy
3. Add salt and allow to ferment overnight

4. The next morning, pour out a ladle full of batter in an '*Appa Chutty*' which is a special wok for making Appam. Lift it up and rotate it so that the batter spreads around and you get a lace like texture

5. Cover the dish with a lid and cook on medium heat
6. Serve hot with Chicken curry or stew

Chicken Curry

Ingredients:

½ kg	–	Chicken with bone (*Kozhi*)
3	–	Onions (*Vengayam*), finely chopped
4	–	Tomatoes (*Thakali*), finely chopped
2 tbsp.	–	Ginger garlic paste (*Inji poondu viluthu*)
½ tsp.	–	Turmeric powder (*Manjal podi*)
2 tbsp.	–	Coriander powder (*Malli podi*)
1 tbsp.	–	Red chili powder (*Milagai podi*)
1" piece	–	Cinnamon stick (*Pattai*)
5	–	Cloves (*Lavangam*)
1 tsp.	–	Cumin seeds (*Seeragam*)
2 sprigs	–	Curry leaves (*Karuvapaellai*), finely chopped
1 cup	–	Coriander leaves (*Kothamali elai*), finely chopped
½ cup	–	Coconut milk (*Thengai paal*)
3 tbsp.	–	Gingelly oil (*Nalla ennai*)
To taste	–	Salt (*Uppu*)
1 cup	–	Buttermilk (*Moru*), for cleaning the chicken

Method:

1. Wash the chicken pieces under running water 3 times. Clean again with buttermilk. This will not only clean the chicken well but also remove any unpleasant odour
2. In a large pot, heat oil
3. Add cinnamon and cloves
4. Add cumin seeds
5. Add onions and sauté well
6. When the onions turn transparent add ginger garlic paste
7. Add curry leaves
8. Add ½ of the coriander leaves
9. Add the chicken pieces
10. Add turmeric powder, coriander powder and red chili powder
11. Add tomato puree and salt
12. Cover and cook on simmer for 15 minutes till the chicken is fully cooked and turns white
13. Add 2 cups of hot water and let it boil
14. Add coconut milk and cook for just 5 minutes
15. Sprinkle the remaining ½ of the coriander leaves on top.

Tip: Dip glass and eversilver vessels in the water in which rice is washed for a few minutes. Then rinse them in cold water for a nice shine. While packing glass plates, place a cardboard or newpaper piece between the plates. Glass tumblers must be stuffed and wrapped with newspapers to prevent breaking.

22. Poori And Potato Curry

Poori

Ingredients:

1 cup	–	Wheat flour (*Gothumai mavu*)
1 tbsp.	–	Gingelly oil (*Nalla ennai*)
To taste	–	Salt (*Uppu*)
3 cups	–	Refined sunflower oil for frying (*Poripathuku ennai*)
1 cup	–	Flour (*Maida mavu*), for dusting

Method:
1. Make dough of wheat flour, salt and water. Water should be sprinkled at intervals and not poured
2. Knead into dough. The dough should not be wet and sticky
3. Add oil and knead again
4. Make small balls
5. Roll out into round pooris, using flour for dusting
6. Fry immediately in very hot oil. The rolled out pooris should not be kept aside for long but fried immediately.
7. Slide the pooris into the hot oil and press one side to puff up the pooris

Potato Curry

Ingredients:

1	–	Potato (*Urulaikkilangu*)
½ cup	–	Peas (*Pattani*)
1	–	Onions (*Vengayam*), finely chopped
2	–	Green chilies (*Pachai milagai*), finely chopped
1	–	Tomatoes (*Thakali*), julienned
½ tsp.	–	Turmeric powder (*Manjal podi*)
1 tsp.	–	Mustard (*Kadugu*)
1 tsp.	–	Bengal gram (*Kadalai parupu*)
3	–	Dry red chilies (*Kanja milagai*), broken into 2

1 sprig	–	Curry leaves (*Karuvapaellai*), finely chopped
½ cup	–	Coriander leaves (*Kothamali elai*), finely chopped
1 tbsp.	–	Gingelly oil (*Nalla ennai*)

Method:
1. Place the potato and peas in 2 separate containers and steam cook in the pressure cooker for 3 whistles
2. Peel the potato and mash well
3. In a wok (*Kadai*), heat oil
4. Season with mustard, bengal gram and dry red chilies
5. Add onions and green chilies
6. Add curry leaves
7. Add tomatoes and peas
8. Add turmeric powder
9. Add the tomato and salt
10. Add the mashed potato and mix well
11. Add 1 cup of water
12. Cover and cook for 10 minutes
13. Add coriander leaves

Tip: To get a nice, puffed up poori, fry the poori immediately in hot oil as soon as it is rolled out. The dough should not be kept aside for a long time especially after rolling out. While frying, press one side of the poori gently with the spoon. The poori will puff up automatically.

23. Rava upma and Kesari

Upma

Ingredients:

1 cup	–	Roasted rava (*Varutha ravai*)
1	–	Onions (*Vengayam*), finely chopped
1	–	Green chili (*Pachai milagai*), finely chopped
1 cup	–	Mixed vegetables (*Kaikarigal*), cubed: carrots, beans, peas
1 tbsp.	–	Bengal gram (*Kadalai parupu*)
1" piece	–	Ginger (*Inji*), grated finely
1 tsp.	–	Mustard (*Kadugu*)
½ tsp.	–	Cumin seeds (*Seeragam*)
8	–	Cashewnuts (*Mundiri*), roasted
2 tbsp.	–	Ghee (*Nei*)
5 tbsp.	–	Gingelly oil (*Nalla ennai*)
1 sprig	–	Curry leaves (*Karuvapaellai*), finely chopped
1 cup	–	Coriander leaves (*Kothamali elai*)
2	–	Lime (*Elumichai pazham*), cut into wedges
3 cups	–	Water

Method:
1. In a large wok (*Kadai*), heat oil and ghee
2. Add mustard.
3. When the mustard splutters, add cumin seeds
4. Add onions and curry leaves finely chopped
5. Add green chilies finely chopped
6. Add cashewnuts
7. Add vegetables and mix well
8. Sprinkle water. Cover and cook under a lid
9. When the vegetables have cooked, add 3 cups of water (Ratio: Rava 1:3 Water)

10. Add salt
11. When the water boils, add rava, stirring continuously to remove lumps
12. Simmer. Cover and cook for 5 minutes under a lid
13. Add freshly cut coriander leaves and mix well
14. Serve hot with sugar or served with a squeeze of lime

Kesari

Ingredients:

1 cup	–	Roasted rava (*Varutha ravai*)
5 tbsp.	–	Ghee (*Nei*)
1 cup	–	Sugar (*Sarkarai*)
½ cup	–	Pineapple pieces (*Annasi pazham*)
12	–	Cashewnuts (*Mundiri*), chopped
½ cup	–	Raisins (*Ularnta thirachai*)
2 tbsp.	–	Refined sunflower oil (*Poripathuku ennai*)
2 tsp.	–	Pineapple essence, for flavor
¼ tsp.	–	Yellow colour
3 cups	–	Water

Method:

1. Heat 2 tbsp. oil and 2 tbsp. ghee in a large wok (*Kadai*)
2. Add pineapple pieces, cashewnuts and after the cashewnuts have roasted for a minute add the raisins. Stir for 2 minutes
3. Add Rava and mix well
4. In a saucepan boil water with a little yellow colour
5. Add the boiling water slowly and carefully to the rava. The water will boil over if added all at once
6. Reduce the flame and stir well. Now cover the wok with a lid and allow the Rava to cook for 8 minutes
7. Increase the flame and add sugar. Mix well so that the sugar dissolves

8. Add the remaining 3 tbsp. ghee
9. Reduce the flame and add pineapple essence
10. The kesari is now ready. It may be runny at the moment but as it cools it will set

Tip: The secret of tasty upma is the overload of ghee and oil that is used for cooking it. Adding more makes it tasty and soft. While making kesari, always fry cashewnuts first and then add raisins as cashewnuts take a longer time to fry than raisins

24. Adai

Ingredients:

½ cup	–	Split red gram (*Thoovaram parupu*)
½ cup	–	Bengal gram (*Kadalai parupu*)
½ cup	–	Green gram (*Pasi parupu*)
½ cup	–	Black gram (*Ullutham parupu*)
½ cup	–	Corn (*Sollam*)
¼ cup	–	Boiled Rice (*Pulangal Arasi*)
⅛ tsp.	–	Asafoetida (*Perungayam*)
4	–	Dry red chilly (*Kanja milagai*), long
2 sprigs	–	Curry leaves (*Karuvapaellai*), finely chopped
½ cup	–	Coriander leaves (*Kothamali elai*), finely chopped

| ¼ cup | – | Grated coconut (*Thuruviya thengai*) |
| As required | – | Ghee (*Nei*), for cooking |

Method:

1. Soak all the dhals and rice overnight
2. Grind to get a thick batter
3. Add grated coconut, finely chopped curry leaves and coriander leaves. Mix well
4. Add asafoetida and salt
5. Take a ladle full of batter and pour out a dosai on a hot tava
6. Add ghee all around and in the center
7. Turn over and cook on the other side also
8. Serve hot with Sambar

Tip: To prevent a glass vessel from cracking when a hot liquid is poured into it, first put a metal spoon into the vessel to absorb the heat. This way the glass vessel will not break, no matter how hot the liquid is.

25. Rava Dosai

Ingredients:

½ cup	–	Roasted Rava (*Varutha ravai*)
1-½ cups	–	Rice flour (*Arasi mavu*)
2 tbsp.	–	Flour (*Maida mavu*)
2 tsp.	–	Peppercorns (*Milagu*)
2 tsp.	–	Cumin seeds (*Seeragam*)
3	–	Green chilies (*Pachai milagai*), finely chopped

1" piece	–	Ginger (*Inji*), finely chopped
2 sprigs	–	Curry leaves (***Karuvapaellai***), finely chopped
To taste	–	Salt (***Uppu***)
As required	–	Ghee (***Nei***), for cooking

Method:

1. Mix all the above ingredients with 4 cups of water. The right consistency of the batter is extremely watery and runny without any lumps
2. Heat a tava to high heat. Only if the tava is extremely hot, will you get the desired lace like texture for the rava dosai
3. Pour out a ladle full of batter on the tava and let it run
4. Smear ghee around the edges and on top. Cooking oil can also be used but the flavor is good with ghee
5. Turn over so that the other side gets cooked too
6. Serve hot with sambar and any chutney

Note:

- The ratio of Rava to Rice flour is 1:3
- Flour is the binding agent
- Optional: add fried cashewnuts or finely chopped onions to get a different flavour

Tip: Rava stays fresh and free from worms if lightly roasted before storing. Rava and flour can be kept free from worms if stored in the refrigerator.

26. Bombay Toast – Sweet and Karam

Sweet

Ingredients:

6 slices	–	Bread (*Rotti*)
2	–	Eggs (*Muttai*)
12 tbsp.	–	Sugar (*Sarkarai*)
½ tsp.	–	Vanilla Essence (*Vanilla saarai*)
1/3 cup	–	Boiled milk (***Kothikavaitha Paal***)
2 tbsp.	–	Ghee (*Nei*)

Method:

1. In a large bowl whisk together all the above ingredients except bread and ghee.

   (**Note**: Use only milk that is at room temperature. Do not use hot milk, as the eggs will scramble in the heat of the milk)

2. Dip the bread slices in the batter one by one so that each slice gets fully soaked with sweetness

3. Smear a hot tava with a little ghee

4. Place the bread slices on the tava and let them cook on medium heat. A high flame is not favoured as it will burn the toast on the outside but the inside will still be raw. A flame on simmer is not favoured as it will harden and dry the toast

5. When the lower side is done, flip the slice over and cook on the other side until caramel brown.

6. Cut the slices along the diagonal into triangles.

Karam

Ingredients:

6 slices	–	Bread (*Rotti*)
2	–	Eggs (*Muttai*)
½	–	Onions (*Vengayam*), finely chopped
½	–	Tomatoes (*Thakali*), finely chopped
¼	–	Capsicum (*Kudai milagai*), finely chopped (*optional*)

1	–	Green chilies (*Pachai milagai*), finely chopped
1 sprig	–	Curry leaves (*Karuvapaellai*), finely chopped
¼ cup	–	Coriander leaves (*Kothamali elai*), finely chopped
½ tsp.	–	Pepper powder (*Milagu thul*)
¼ tsp.	–	Turmeric powder (*Manjal podi*)
½ tsp.	–	Red chili powder (*Milagai podi*)
2 tbsp.	–	Butter (*Vennai*)
To taste	–	Salt (*Uppu*)

Method:

1. In a large bowl, whisk together all the above ingredients except butter and bread
2. Dip the bread slices in the batter one by one so that each slice gets fully soaked
3. Smear a hot tava with a little butter
4. Place the bread slices on the tava and let them cook on medium heat. A high flame is not favoured as it will burn the toast on the outside but the inside will still be raw. A flame on simmer is not favoured as it will harden and dry the toast
5. When the lower side is done, flip the slice over and cook on the other side until the eggs cook like an omelette.
6. Remove from the fire and grate mozzarella cheese (optional) on top. Cut the slices along the diagonal into triangles. Serve hot with tomato ketchup

Tip: Vanilla essence is added to remove the unpleasant smell of eggs in the *Sweet Bombay toast* whereas Pepper is added to remove the smell of eggs in the *Karam Bombay toast*

27. Idly, Dosai & Coconut Chutney

Ingredients:

1 cup	–	Black gram (*Ullutham parupu*)
4 cups	–	Idly rice (*Idly arisi*)
2 tbsp.	–	Boiled rice (*Pulangal Arasi*)
1 tbsp.	–	Fenugreek seeds (*Vendayam*)
To taste	–	Salt (*Uppu*)
As required	–	Ghee (*Nei*), for greasing the idly trays

Method:

1. Soak Black gram and Boiled rice together overnight or for 8 hours
2. Soak Idly rice and vendayam overnight or for 8 hours
3. Grind each mixture separately in the grinder using the same water used for soaking
4. Mix both batters together
5. Refrigerate the batter. Every day take out only the desired amount to be used and keep outside for fermenting.
6. Add salt

Idly

1. To make idlies, boil a little water in the idly cooker
2. Grease the idly trays with a little ghee

3. Pour out a ladle full of batter in each idly cup
4. When the water boils, put the stacks of idly trays in the cooker. Never put it when the water is cold
5. Cover and cook for 7 minutes
6. Let it rest for 3 minutes before taking the trays out
7. Scoop out each idly carefully
8. Serve hot with sambar, vadai and a variety of chutneys

Dosai

1. Pour out a ladle full of batter on a hot tava
2. Spread out the batter in concentric circles using the back of the ladle
3. Drizzle ghee or oil around the edges and in the centre
4. Place a lid on top and let it steam cook for 3 minutes
5. Serve hot with potato curry, sambar and coconut chutney

Coconut Chutney

Ingredients:

4 tbsp.	–	Grated coconut (*Thuruviya thengai*)
1 tsp.	–	Tamarind paste (*Puli*)
1	–	Green chili (*Pachai milagai*)
1	–	Garlic (*Poondu*)
½ tsp.	–	Cumin seeds (*Seeragam*)
½ tsp.	–	Mustard (*Kadugu*)
½ tsp.	–	Black gram (*Ullutham parupu*)
1 sprig	–	Curry leaves (*Karuvapaellai*)
2	–	Dry red chilly, round (*Kanja milagai*)
¾ cup	–	Hot water (*Venneer*)
1 tbsp.	–	Gingelly Oil (*Nalla ennai*)
½ tsp.	–	Ghee (*Nei*)

Method:

1. Grind together grated coconut, tamarind paste, green chili, garlic, cumin seeds and salt in the mixer
2. Add hot water and grind again
3. In a seasoning pan, heat oil and ghee
4. Season with mustard
5. When the mustard starts spluttering, add black gram, curry leaves and dry red chilly
6. Pour this into the ground chutney and mix well

Tip: While making idlies grease the idly tray with oil or ghee, before pouring the batter into it. This will help you to remove the idlies easily after cooking. In case you do not have an idly tray, small tumblers can be used to make '*tumbler idly*'!!!

28. Puttu

Ingredients:

1 cup	–	Rice flour (*Arasi mavu*)
½ tsp.	–	Salt (*Uppu*)
¾ cup	–	Warm Water
¼ cup	–	Grated coconut (*Thuruviya thengai*)

Method:

1. In a deep bowl combine rice flour and salt
2. Sprinkle water and mix in till the mixture resembles breadcrumbs.
3. To ensure there are no lumps, pass the rice flour mix through a sieve and flatten out all lumps
4. In a puttu maker or puttu kudam, add a little grated coconut as the first layer
5. Add the prepared rice flour mix till halfway
6. Add a layer of grated coconut

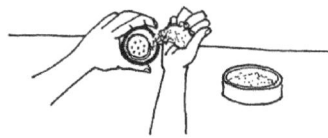

7. Fill the remaining top half of the kudam with the rice flour mix
8. Add the last layer of grated coconut at the top and cover with the lid
9. Heat water in the kudam pot
10. When the water starts boiling, place the kudam on top. The puttu will cook in the steam generated by the boiling water in about 5 minutes

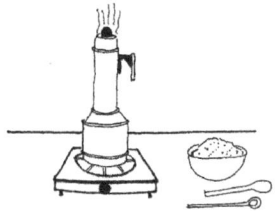

11. Remove and keep aside
12. After 5 minutes, use the pin to push out the puttu onto a place for serving

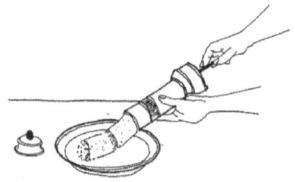

13. Puttu tastes best when eaten with sugar and bananas, but can also be eaten with ripe mangoes or *Brown chickpeas curry*

Tip: To check if a coconut is good or has gone bad, shake it. If there is a sound of coconut water inside, the coconut is good. If it is dry, the coconut has gone bad. Grated coconut can be preserved for a longer time if stored in a plastic container in the freezer

29. Pancake

Ingredients:

½ cup	–	Flour (*Maida mavu*)
1	–	Eggs (*Muttai*)
6 tbsp.	–	Sugar (*Sarkarai*) or to desired sweetness
½ cup	–	Boiled milk (*Kothikavaitha Paal*)
½ tsp.	–	Vanilla essence (*Vanilla saarai*)
A pinch	–	Baking Soda (*Aapa soda*)
To taste	–	Salt (*Uppu*)
As required	–	Ghee (*Nei*) or else use Butter (*Vennai*)

Method:
1. Whisk the egg well with sugar
2. Add milk
3. Add vanilla essence
4. Add flour sifted with baking soda and mix well to get a smooth batter and to remove any lumps
5. Add a pinch of salt
6. On a flat tava, pour out a ladle full of batter
7. Add a tsp. of butter or ghee all around. Simmer and cook
8. Flip over and cook on both sides
9. Serve hot with jam or chocolate sauce

Tip: Add 3 tbsp. of cocoa powder to the basic pancake batter to get *Chocolate pancakes*. Another variation is adding 1 mashed banana to the basic pancake batter to get *Banana pancake*.

30. Pongal – Sweet and Ven

Sweet Pongal
Ingredients:

1-½ cup	–	Raw rice (*Pacha arasi*)
¼ cup	–	Green gram (*Pasi parupu*)
8 cups	–	Boiled milk (*Kothikavaitha Paal*)
1-½ cups	–	Jagggery (*Vellam*)
¼ cup	–	Water to dissolve the jaggery

15	–	Cashewnuts (*Mundiri*)
10	–	Almonds ((*Badam parupu*)
30	–	Raisins (*Ularnta thirachai*)
1 tbsp.	–	Saffron (*Kungumapu*)
1 tbsp.	–	Cardamom powder (*Elakai thul*)
6 tbsp.	–	Ghee (*Nei*)

Method:
1. Heat jaggery with a little water. When it dissolves, strain the jaggery water and keep aside. This is to remove dirt and impurities, if any
2. Pour milk in a large pot and let it boil
3. When it starts boiling, add the rice and dhal
4. Let it cook to softness
5. Add jaggery water
6. Add 4 tbsp. of ghee and let it cook further on medium heat
7. In a seasoning pan, take 2 tbsp. of ghee. Lighly fry cashewnuts, almonds. Remove and keep aside. Now fry the raisins
8. Add all this to the pot
9. Add saffron dissolved in a little milk
10. Bring the pongal to a boil. Remove and serve hot. The pongal may be runny when hot but will harden with time.

Ven Pongal

Ingredients:

½ cup	–	Raw rice (*Pacha arasi*)
¼ cup	–	Green gram (*Pasi parupu*)
½ tsp.	–	Asafoetida (*Perungayam*)
1 tsp.	–	Mustard (*Kadugu*)
1 tsp.	–	Cumin seeds (*Seeragam*)
1 tbsp.	–	Peppercorns (*Milagu*)
1 tbsp.	–	Ginger, grated (*Milagu*)
¼ tsp.	–	Turmeric powder (*Manjal podi*)
7	–	Cashewnuts (*Mundiri*)

¼ cup	–	Boiled milk (*Kothikavaitha Paal*)
1 sprig	–	Curry leaves (*Karuvapaellai*)
1 tbsp.	–	Gingelly oil (*Nalla ennai*)
3 tbsp	–	Ghee (*Nei*)
To taste	–	Salt (*Uppu*)

Method:

1. In a wok (*Kadai*), lightly roast raw rice and green gram together till you get a nice aroma
2. In a pressure cooker, boil together the roasted rice and gram along with asafoetida and 2-¼ cups of water (Ratio – 1:3) for 4 whistles
3. Remove the cooked rice and dhal from heat and mash well.
4. Add milk and mix well
5. In a wok (*Kadai*), heat oil and 2 tbsp. of ghee
6. Season with mustard
7. When the mustard splutters, add cumin seeds and curry leaves
8. Add grated ginger and peppercorns
9. Add turmeric powder
10. Add this seasoning to the rice and mix well. The **Ven Pongal** is ready.
11. Transfer to the serving bowl. Spread 1 tbsp. of ghee on top of the pongal and cover the bowl with a lid to retain all the nice flavours until serving time. The pongal may be runny when hot but it will thicken and settle as it cools.
12. Serve **Ven Pongal** with **Sambar** and **Tomato chutney**

Tip: When boiling potatoes or eggs, adding salt to the water before boiling, helps to peel the skin easily later

Lunch Box

*"The heart of her husband doth safely trust in her,
so that he shall have no need of spoil.
She will do him good and not evil all the days of her life"*

(Proverbs 31:11,12)

Lunch box recipes are those that are prepared hot but eaten cold. Hence, packing the perfect lunch box for your husband and children can be a task most challenging. Food packed into a lunch box should be easy to make at the crack of dawn and yet healthy, nutritious and tasty! It has to be preferably dry and a non-spill, non-messy dish which can be packed in a box. The dish should be spoon-eatable and hence boneless. Considering all this, it's easy to run out of ideas and pack the age-old boring lunch sandwich or worse still, end up packing the same dish day after day. But it does n't have to be like that at all. There are countless lunch box recipes and I have presented a few here.

A lunch box is like a surprise gift that you pack for your husband and kids. At school or at work, when it is opened, the contents of the lunch box must make them smile. It is also the unseen way your husband and kids introduce you to their collegues and classmates. So take extra care in planning and preparing an impressive, good lunch box for your loved ones. I dedicate this section to my husband and daughter for whom I lovingly pack a lunch box every day.

Carrying a lunch box was part of my school days. Now, decades later, quite surprisingly I do not remember my classmates according to the grade they scored in exams but rather by the lunch box they carried to school! Lunchtime at school was a like a potluck when tiffin boxes would be opened and we would all have a love feast of different varieties of lunches. Thanks to my mom for making my life so good with so many delicious lunch box dishes.

Notes: I have shared a few do's and don't's from my experience:

- o I would advise you not to pack ghee rice for lunch as the ghee solidifies and does not taste nice when cold. Ghee rice must be eaten hot as soon as it is prepared.

- Any dish with egg in it is not advisable for the lunch box, such as egg-fried rice or egg noodles as it does not remain fresh when packed.
- Never pack the tiffin box when the food is hot unless it is a hot pack or casserole. Wait till the food has coolled down to room temperature and then close the lid.

31. Chapati and Potato Poriyal

Chapati

Ingredients:

2 cups	–	Wheat flour (*Gothumai mavu*)
To taste	–	Salt (*Uppu*)
1 tbsp. + ½ cup	–	Gingelly oil (*Nalla ennai*)
½ cup	–	Flour (*Maida mavu*), for dusting

Method:

1. Knead wheat flour and salt into a wet dough by sprinkling warm water. Do not pour

2. Add 1 tbsp. of gingelly oil and knead again

3. Shape into medium size balls

4. Roll out into round chapatis on a board, dusting in flour.

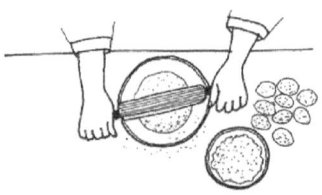

5. Cook on a hot tava till light brown spots appear
6. Smear with oil

7. Place a tea towel in a casserole. Pile up the chapatis in the towel and keep it closed. Cover the casserole to keep the chapatis soft and warm

Potato Poriyal

Ingredients:

1	–	Potato (*Urulaikkilangu*)
½ cup	–	Peas (*Pattani*)
1	–	Onions (*Vengayam*), julienned
1	–	Tomatoes (*Thakali*), julienned
½ tsp.	–	Turmeric powder (*Manjal podi*)
1 tsp.	–	Coriander powder (*Malli podi*)
1 tsp.	–	Red chili powder (*Milagai podi*)
¼ tsp.	–	Garam masala (*Garam masala podi*)

1 tsp.	–	Mustard (*Kadugu*)
1 tsp.	–	Cumin seeds (*Seeragam*)
1 sprig	–	Curry leaves (*Karuvapaellai*), finely chopped
½ cup	–	Coriander leaves (*Kothamali elai*), finely chopped
3 tbsp.	–	Gingelly Oil (*Nalla ennai*)

Method:

1. Place the potato in 1 container and the peas in another container. Steam cook in the pressure cooker for 3 whistles
2. Peel the potato and mash well
3. In a wok, heat oil
4. Season with mustard and cumin seeds
5. Add onions and sauté well
6. Add curry leaves
7. Add the cooked peas
8. Add turmeric powder, coriander powder, red chili powder and garam masala
9. Add the tomato and salt
10. Add the mashed potato and mix well
11. Cover and cook for 10 minutes
12. Add coriander leaves and remove from heat

Tip: Aluminium foil is the best for keeping chapatti dough soft and for a long time in the refrigerator. It is also the best for keeping sandwiches fresh or biscuits crisp.

32. Chicken Katti Roll

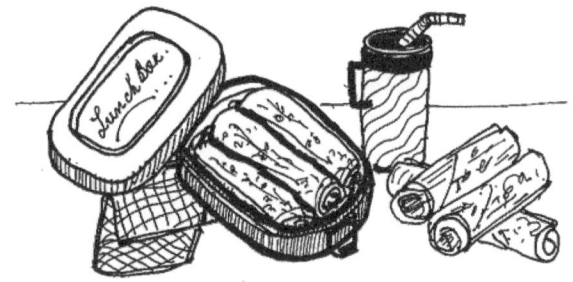

Ingredients:
Dough:

1 cup	–	Wheat flour (*Gothumai mavu*)
½ cup	–	Flour (*Maida mavu*)
¾ tsp.	–	Salt (*Uppu*)
1 tbsp.	–	Gingelly oil (*Nalla ennai*)
1	–	Egg (*Muttai*)
1 cup	–	Warm water, for kneading
4	–	Eggs (*Muttai*) for layering the roll

Filling:

250 g	–	Boneless chicken (*Kozhi*), shredded
1 tsp.	–	Cumin seeds (*Seeragam*)
1	–	Onions (*Vengayam*), finely chopped
½	–	Capsicum (*Kudai milagai*), finely chopped
1 tbsp.	–	Ginger garlic paste (*Inji poondu viluthu*)
1	–	Tomatoes (*Thakali*), finely chopped
¼ tsp.	–	Turmeric powder (*Manjal podi*)
1 tsp.	–	Coriander powder (*Malli podi*)
2 tsp.	–	Red chili powder (*Milagai podi*)
½ tsp.	–	Garam masala (*Garam masala podi*)
1 tsp.	–	Chaat masala (*Chaat masala podi*)
1 cup	–	Coriander leaves (*Kothamali elai*)
1	–	Lime juice (*Elumichai saaru*)
3 tbsp.	–	Gingelly Oil (*Nalla ennai*)
To taste	–	Salt (*Uppu*)

Method:
1. In a large pan, heat 3 tbsp. of oil
2. Add cumin seeds
3. Add onions and capsicum. Saute till they cook
4. Add ginger garlic paste
5. Add tomatoes and salt. Let the tomatoes soften and cook
6. Add the shredded chicken and mix well
7. Add turmeric powder, coriander powder and red chili powder (or you can use 3 tsp. of chicken 65 masala)

8. Simmer. Cover the pan with a lid and let the chicken cook well
9. Add garam masala, chaat masala and salt
10. Remove from heat and add coriander leaves
11. Squeeze a lime over the chicken and toss everything together. This is the filling for the katti roll. Keep aside
12. Combine flour, wheat flour and salt. Rub in 1 tbsp. of oil. Break an egg into it and mix again
13. Sprinkle a little water and knead into a soft dough
14. Divide the dough into about 8 balls
15. Roll out like rotis
16. Place on a hot tava and allow it to cook till light brown spots start to appear. Flip over and allow the other side to cook
17. Beat the eggs well and pour out half an egg over the roti. Smear it all over the roti.
18. Flip the roti over to cook the egg for a couple of minutes. Drizzle oil all around
19. Remove from heat. Place a little chicken filling inside the roti. Roll up well to ensure the filling does not spill out
20. Wrap with foil to keep warm and place in the tiffin box

Tip: Raw meat and vegetables are easier to cut if the knife is dipped in boiling water first

33. Coconut Rice and Valaka Fry

Ingredients:

½	–	Grated coconut (*Thuruviya thengai*)
3 cups	–	Cooked rice (*Sadam*)
12	–	Cashewnuts (*Mundiri*), halved
½ tsp.	–	Mustard (*Kadugu*)
1 tbsp.	–	Broken black gram (*Ullutham parupu*)
1 tbsp.	–	Black gram (*Kadalai parupu*)
4	–	Dry red chili (*Kanja milagai*)
A pinch	–	Asafoetida (*Perungayam*)
1	–	Lime juice (*Elumichai saaru*)
3 tbsp.	–	Gingelly oil (*Nalla ennai*)
1 tbsp.	–	Ghee (*Nei*)
To taste	–	Salt (*Uppu*)

Method:
1. Boil the rice and leave aside to cool
2. In a large pot, heat 3 oil
3. Season with mustard, urad dhal, kadala parupu, curry leaves and kanja milagai
4. Fry grated coconut lightly
5. Toss in the cooked rice and salt. Mix well
6. Fry cashewnuts in ghee and add to the rice

Tip: Add 2 tbsp. of idly podi for enhanced flavor and taste (optional)

Side Dish: Valaka Fry

Ingredients:

2	–	Raw banana (*Valaka*)
1 tbsp.	–	Ginger garlic paste (*Inji poondu viluthu*)
1 tsp.	–	Turmeric powder (*Manjal podi*)
2 tbsp.	–	Coriander powder (*Malli podi*)
2 tbsp.	–	Red chili powder (*Milagai podi*)
1 tbsp.	–	Corn flour (*Solla mavu*)
To taste	–	Salt (*Uppu*)
½ cup	–	Refined sunflower oil for shallow frying (*Poripathuku ennai*)

Method:
1. Peel the raw banana and slice into thick rounds
2. Make a thick paste of ginger garlic paste, turmeric powder, coriander powder, red chili powder and corn flour with a little water
3. Smear over all the rounds on both sides
4. Keep aside for 20 minutes in the refrigerator
5. Heat oil in a pan
6. Shallow fry the raw banana. Turn over and cook as soon as one side cooks
7. Remove and drain the oil on oil absorbent paper

Tip: As soon as you cut the raw banana, dip the slices in cold water to prevent blackening

34. Lemon Rice and Chicken Masala

Ingredients:
1 cup	–	Boiled Rice (*Pulangal Arasi*), uncooked
1	–	Lime juice (*Elumichai saaru*)
½ tsp.	–	Turmeric powder (*Manjal podi*)
1	–	Garlic (*Poondu*)
1 tsp.	–	Mustard (*Kadugu*)
½ tsp.	–	Black gram (*Ullutham parupu*)
½ tsp.	–	Bengal gram (*Kadala parupu*)
2 sprigs	–	Curry leaves (*Karuvapaellai*)
¼ cup	–	Groundnuts (*Ver kadalai*)

4	–	Red dry chilies (*Kanja milagai*), broken into bits
3 tbsp.	–	Gingelly oil (*Nal Ennai*)
To taste	–	Salt (*Uppu*)

Method:
1. Cook the rice till it is tender, strain water and keep aside
2. Heat oil in a wok
3. Season with mustard seeds, bengal gram and black gram
4. When these turn a little brown in colour, add red dry chilies and stir well
5. Add garlic and curry leaves
6. Stir well and keep on flame for two minutes
7. Add pre-boiled rice and salt
8. Add lemon juice and salt. Mix well
9. Keep on flame for another 3 minutes before serving

Side Dish: Chicken Masala

Ingredients:

¼ kg	–	Boneless chicken (*Kozhi*), cubed
1	–	Onions (*Vengayam*), finely chopped
2	–	Tomatoes (*Thakali*), finely chopped
4	–	Cloves (*Krambu*)
1	–	Cinnamon stick (*Pattai*)
1 tsp.	–	Cumin seeds (*Seeragam*)
1 tbsp.	–	Ginger garlic paste (*Inji poondu viluthu*)
1 cup	–	Coriander leaves (*Kothamali elai*), finely chopped
½ tsp.	–	Turmeric powder (*Manjal podi*)
1 tbsp.	–	Coriander powder (*Malli podi*)
1 tbsp.	–	Red chili powder (*Milagai podi*)
1	–	Lime juice (*Elumichai saaru*)
3 tbsp.	–	Gingelly oil (*Nalla ennai*)
To taste	–	Salt (*Uppu*)

Method:
1. In a wok, heat oil
2. Add cloves, cinnamon and cumin seeds
3. Add onions
4. When the onions turn transparent, add ginger garlic paste
5. Add ½ cup of coriander leaves
6. Add turmeric powder, coriander powder and red chili powder
7. After 2 minutes, add the tomatoes and salt.
8. Add the chicken and mix well
9. Cover the wok and let the chicken cook for 15 minutes
10. Just before serving, add lime juice and ½ cup of coriander leaves. Mix well

Tip: Wash the chicken under running water 2 times. Soak in curds or buttermilk for 20 minutes. Now wash again under running water. This will clean the chicken well and remove unpleasant odour, if any

35. Sambar Rice and Chicken Pakoda

Ingredients:
1 cup	–	Boiled Rice (*Pulangal Arasi*), uncooked
½ cup	–	Red gram (*Thoovaram parupu*)
8	–	Shallots (*Sambar vengayam*) full, not chopped
2	–	Brinjals (*Katharikai*), chopped

1	–	Carrot (*Manjal mulangi*), cubed
6	–	Beans (*Vithayavarai*), cubed
2	–	Drumsticks (*Murungakai*)
1 tbsp.	–	Tamarind paste (*Puli saaru*)
2	–	Green chilies (*Pachai milagai*), broken into two
½ tsp.	–	Turmeric powder (*Manjal podi*)
2 tbsp.	–	Sambar powder (*Sambar podi*)
¼ tsp.	–	Asafoetida (*Perungayam*)
1 tsp.	–	Mustard (*Kadugu*)
1 tsp.	–	Black gram (*Ullutham parupu*)
10	–	Cashewnuts (*Mundiri*)
2 sprigs	–	Curry leaves (*Karuvapaellai*)
½ cup	–	Coriander leaves (*Kothamali elai*), finely chopped
2 tbsp.	–	Ghee (*Nei*)
2 tbsp.	–	Gingelly oil (*Nalla ennai*)
To taste	–	Salt (*Uppu*)

Method:

1. Soak 1 lime size piece of tamarind in 2 cups of hot water for 10 minutes. Squeeze out the tamarind to get exract. Or else use tamarind paste
2. Heat 1 tbsp. oil and 1 tbsp. ghee in the pressure cooker
3. Saute shallots and green chilies
4. Add asafoetida
5. Add all the vegetables and fry lightly for 10 minutes
6. Add turmeric powder, sambar powder and salt. Mix well
7. Add red gram and rice
8. Add 2 cups of tamarind extract. Cover and cook for 3 whistles
9. In a large wok, heat 1 tbsp. oil and 1 tbsp. ghee
10. Add mustard
11. When the mustard splutters, add black gram
12. Add curry leaves
13. Add this tempering to the rice. Add salt and mix well

Side Dish: Chicken Pakoda

Ingredients:

1 cup	–	Cooked and shredded chicken (*Kozhi*)
1 cup	–	Bengal gram flour (*Kadala mavu*)
¼ cup	–	Rice flour (*Arasi mavu*)
¼ tsp.	–	Baking soda (*Aapa soda*)
½ tbsp.	–	Ghee (*Nei*)
8	–	Cashewnuts (*Mundiri*), chopped
1	–	Onions (*Vengayam*), finely chopped
1	–	Green chilies (*Pachai milagai*), finely chopped
¼ tsp.	–	Turmeric powder (*Manjal podi*)
1 tsp.	–	Coriander powder (*Malli podi*)
1 tsp.	–	Red chili powder (*Milagai podi*)
1 tbsp.	–	Ginger garlic paste (*Inji poondu viluthu*)
2 sprigs	–	Curry leaves (*Karuvapaellai*), finely chopped
3 cups	–	Refined sunflower oil for frying (*Poripathuku ennai*)
To taste	–	Salt (*Uppu*)

Method:

1. Heat 2 tbsp. oil in a wok
2. Saute onions and green chilies
3. Add ginger garlic paste
4. Add the cooked and shredded chicken pieces
5. Add salt
6. Add turmeric powder, coriander powder and red chili powder (or else use 2 tbsp. of chicken masala)
7. Add cashewnuts and curry leaves
8. Remove from heat and allow to cool a little
9. Add Bengal gram flour mixed with rice flour and baking soda
10. Sprinkle a little water and mix well to get a semi-dry batter
11. Check for salt and add more if needed

12. Take rugged spoonfulls of the mix and drop into hot oil
13. Deep fry till golden brown. Drain on absorbent paper

Tip: To prevent rice and dhals from insects, dry them in the hot sun after buying. In case there are insects, pass them through a medium sized sieve to remove the insects. In the rice tin, place a few neem leaves at the bottom and then store the rice This will keep away insects.

36. Pepper Rice and Mutton Masala

Ingredients:

2 cups	–	Cooked rice (*Sadam*)
2 tbsp.	–	Pepper corns (*Milagu*)
1 tsp. + 1 tsp.	–	Black gram (*Ullutham parupu*)
1 tsp. + 1 tsp.	–	Bengal gram (*Kadalai parupu*)
12	–	Cashew nuts (*Mundiri*), ground coarsely
1 sprig	–	Curry leaves (*Karuvapaellai*), finely chopped
1 tbsp.	–	Ghee (*Nei*)
1 tbsp.	–	Gingelly oil (*Nalla ennai*)
To taste	–	Salt (*Uppu*)

Method:

1. Heat oil in a wok
2. Roast 1 tbsp. of pepper corns, 1 tsp. black gram and 1 tsp. Bengal gram till they redden and you get a nice aroma. Remove from heat
3. Cool and grind to a fine powder
4. Heat ghee in a large wok
5. Add 1 tbsp. of pepper corns, 1 tsp. black gram and 1 tsp. Bengal gram
6. Add cashewnuts

7. Add the cooked rice and salt
8. Add curry leaves and mix well

Side Dish: Mutton Masala

Ingredients:

¼ kg	–	Boneless mutton (*Aattu kari*), cubed
1	–	Potato (*Urulaikkilangu*), cubed
2	–	Onions (*Vengayam*), finely chopped
2	–	Tomatoes (*Thakali*), finely chopped
4	–	Cloves (*Krambu*)
1	–	Cinnamon stick (*Pattai*)
1 tsp.	–	Fennel seeds (*Sombu*)
1 tsp.	–	Cumin seeds (*Seeragam*)
1 tbsp.	–	Ginger garlic paste (*Inji poondu viluthu*)
2 sprigs	–	Curry leaves (*Karuvapaellai*), finely chopped
½ tsp.	–	Turmeric powder (*Manjal podi*)
1 tbsp.	–	Coriander powder (*Malli podi*)
1 tbsp.	–	Red chili powder (*Milagai podi*)
3 tbsp.	–	Gingelly oil (*Nalla ennai*)
To taste	–	Salt (*Uppu*)

Method:

1. Boil the mutton in a pressure cooker for 8 whistles with turmeric powder, salt and enough water to cover the mutton
2. In a wok, heat the oil
3. Add cloves, cinnamon and fennel seeds
4. Saute onions till they turn slightly brown
5. Add curry leaves
6. Add ginger garlic paste
7. Add turmeric powder, coriander powder and red chili powder
8. Add the potato cubes
9. After 2 minutes, add the tomatoes and salt.
10. Add the pre-boiled mutton and mix well
11. Cover the wok and for 10 minutes

Tip: To make ginger-garlic paste grind two parts of ginger to one part of garlic. To preserve it for a long time, add a little oil and salt while grinding but take utmost care not to add any water while grinding. Store in small plastic containers in the freezer. Use whenever needed

37. Mango Rice and Prawn Fry

Ingredients:

1 cup	–	Boiled rice (*Pulangal Arasi*), uncooked
1	–	Raw mango (*Thuriviya mangai*), de-skinned and grated
1 tsp.	–	Mustard (*Kadugu*)
5	–	Dry red chili (*Kanja milagai*)
10	–	Garlic (*Poondu*)
1 tsp.	–	Black gram (*Ullutham parupu*)
1 tsp.	–	Bengal gram (*Kadalai parupu*)
5	–	Cashew nuts (*Mundiri*), halved
2 sprigs	–	Curry leaves (*Karuvapaellai*)
¼ tsp.	–	Turmeric powder (*Manjal podi*)
2 tbsp.	–	Gingelly oil (*Nalla ennai*)
1 tbsp.	–	Ghee (*Nei*)
To taste	–	Salt (*Uppu*)

Method:

1. Cook the rice and keep aside
2. In a large wok, heat oil

3. Season with mustard, urad dhal, kadala parupu
4. Add kanja milagain broken into bits
5. Add garlic
6. Add the grated mango
7. Add turmeric powder and salt
8. Sprinkle water and let the mango cook
9. Toss in the cooked rice and mix well
10. Fry cashewnuts in ghee and add to the rice. Mix well

Side Dish: Prawn Fry

Ingredients:

2 cups	–	Prawns (*Eral meen*), de-shelled
½ tsp.	–	Turmeric powder (*Manjal podi*)
1 tbsp.	–	Coriander powder (*Malli podi*)
2 tbsp.	–	Red chili powder (*Milagai podi*)
2	–	Lime juice (*Elumichai saaru*)
½ cup	–	Curds (*Thayir*), for cleaning
To taste	–	Salt (*Uppu*)
2 cups	–	Refined sunflower oil for frying (*Poripathuku ennai*)

Method:

1. Shell the prawns and de-vein them.
2. Clean the prawns under running water 2 times
3. Soak the prawns in ½ cup of curds for 10 minutes. This will remove all the odour from the prawns. Wash again with water.
4. Make a thick marinade of turmeric powder, coriander powder, red chili powder, salt and lime juice
5. Marinate the prawns with the paste and keep aside for 20 minutes in the refrigerator
6. Deep fry in hot oil
7. Drain the oil on oil absorbent paper and serve

Tip: Garlic and shallots can be peeled easily if soaked in a bowl of cold water one hour before

38. Peas & Soya Pulao

Ingredients:

1 cup	–	Basmati Rice (*Basmati arisi*), uncooked
2 cups	–	Water
1 cup	–	Peas (*Pattani*)
1 cup	–	Soya Granules (*Soya*)
¼ tsp.	–	Turmeric powder (*Manjal podi*)
1 tsp.	–	Coriander powder (*Malli podi*)
1 tsp.	–	Garam Masala (*Garam masala podi*)
1	–	Onions (*Vengayam*), julienned
5	–	Garlic (*Poondu*), crushed
1	–	Tomatoes (*Thakali*), julienned
5	–	Dry red chilly (*Kanja milagai*)
1	–	Bay leaf (*Brinji elai*)
1" piece	–	Cinnamon (*Pattai*)
3	–	Cardamon (*Elakai*)
4	–	Cloves (*Krambu*)
3 tbsp.	–	Ghee (*Nei*)
To taste	–	Salt (*Uppu*)

Method:

1. Soak the rice for 20 minutes.
2. Drain the water. Lightly toss the rice in 1 tbsp. of ghee for 1 minute till it coats the rice
3. Soak Soya granules in hot boiling wate for 10 minutes. Squeeze out the water and keep aside

4. In the pressure cooker, heat 2 tbsp. of ghee
5. Add the spices – cinnamon, cardamom, cloves and bay leaf
6. Add Dry red chilly
7. Add onions
8. As the onions start to brown slightly, add the crushed garlic
9. Add tomatoes and salt
10. Add turmeric powder and coriander powder
11. Add peas and soya granules. Mix well
12. Add Garam Masala
13. Add warm water
14. When the water starts to boil add the rice
15. Pressure cook for three whistles

Tip: To prevent a crust from forming at the base of an aluminium pressure cooker, add a little limejuice to the water at the base before cooking. For an eversilver pressure cooker, add a little tamarind. This will keep the inside of the pressure cooker shiny and new.

39. Spinach Pulao and Chicken Nuggets

Ingredients:

2 cups	–	Basmati rice (*Basmati arisi*), uncooked
1 cup	–	Spinach leaves (*Any Keerai variety*)
1 tbsp.	–	Butter (*Vennai*)
3	–	Green chilies (*Pachai milagai*), finely chopped

1	–	Onions (*Vengayam*), julienned
½ cup	–	Boiled milk (*Kothikavaitha Paal*)
1 tsp.	–	Cumin seeds (*Seeragam*)
1 tbsp.	–	Ghee (*Nei*)
To taste	–	Salt (*Uppu*)

Method:
1. Heat ghee in a wok
2. Add the rice and fry in the ghee for 1 minute to coat the rice. Remove and keep aside
3. Heat butter in a the pressure cooker
4. Add cumin seeds
5. Saute onions and green chilies
6. Add spinach leaves
7. Add ½ cup of milk
8. Add the rice
9. Add 3-½ cups of water
10. Close the cooker and cook for 3 whistles

Side Dish: Chicken Nuggets

Ingredients:

¼ kg	–	Fillet or boneless chicken breast (*Kozhi*)
½ tsp.	–	Turmeric powder (*Manjal podi*)
1 tsp.	–	Coriander powder (*Malli podi*)
1 tsp.	–	Red chili powder (*Milagai podi*)
1 tbsp.	–	Ginger garlic paste (*Inji poondu viluthu*)
1 tbsp.	–	Chicken masala
1 cup	–	Bread crumbs (*Rotti thul*)
1	–	Egg white (*Muttai venkaru*)
To taste	–	Salt (*Uppu*)
3 cups	–	Refined sunflower oil For frying (*Poripathuku ennai*)

Method:
1. Cut the fillet into finger size pieces
2. Make a marinade with ginger garlic paste, turmeric powder, coriander powder, red chili powder, chicken masala and salt
3. Marinate the chicken fingers with the marinade
4. Dip each finger in well beaten egg white
5. Roll over in bread crumbs
6. Deep fry in hot oil

Tip: An aluminium vessel which has been badly burnt inside can be cleaned easily by boiling an onion in a little water in the pan. This loosens the burnt matter which floats to the top. Remove it and rinse the vessel clean with soap water

40. Fried Rice and Gobi Manchurian

Ingredients:
1 cup	–	Basmati Rice (*Basmati arisi*), uncooked
1	–	Onions (*Vengayam*), julienned
½	–	Capsicum, julienned (*Kudai milagai*)
½ cup	–	Cauliflower florets (*Poo ghoz*)
4	–	Beans (*Vithayavarai*), cut long
1	–	Carrots (*Manjal mulangi*), cut into long strips
½ cup	–	Peas (*Pattani*)
4	–	Garlic (*Poondu*), chopped

1 tsp.	–	White pepper powder (*Vellai milagu podi*)
5	–	Onion stalk (*Vengaya taal*), finely chopped
3	–	Green chilies (*Pachai milagai*), finely chopped
1 tsp.	–	Cumin seeds (*Seeragam*)
1 cup	–	Coriander leaves (*Kothamali elai*), finely chopped
3 tbsp.	–	Fried rice masala
¼ cup	–	Raisins and cashewnuts (*Ularnta thirachai, Mundiri*)
2 tbsp.	–	Ghee (*Nei*)
2 tbsp.	–	Gingelly Oil (*Nalla ennai*)
To taste	–	Salt (*Uppu*)

Method:
1. Cook the rice with water. Remove and keep aside to cool
2. Steam cook the vegetables such as carrots, beans, peas and cauliflower in a steamer or pressure cooker. Remove and keep aside to cool
3. Heat oil and 1 tbsp. ghee in a large wok
4. Add cumin seeds
5. Saute onions and green chilies
6. Add capsicum and onion stalk
7. Add garlic
8. Add all the vegetables and fry lightly.
9. Add fried rice masala. (This step is optional and can be skipped In case you do not have fried rice masala)
10. Toss in the cooked rice
11. Sprinkle salt and pepper powder. Mix well
12. Add raisins and cashewnuts lightly fried in 1 tbsp. of ghee
13. Add coriander leaves. Mix well

Side Dish: Gobi Manchurian

Ingredients:

1	–	Cauliflower (*Poo ghoz*), cut into small florets
¾ cup	–	Flour (*Maida mavu*)
1 tbsp.	–	Corn flour (*Solla mavu*)
2	–	Dry red chilies (*Kanja milagai*), broken
1	–	Green chili (*Pachai milagai*), chopped
¼ tsp.	–	Red chili powder (*Milagai podi*)
1 tbsp. + 1 tbsp.	–	Ginger garlic paste (*Inji poondu viluthu*)
3	–	Garlic (*Poondu*), finely chopped
1 cup	–	Spring onions (*Vasanda vengayam*), finely chopped
1	–	Capsicum (*Kudai milagai*), cubed
¼ tsp.	–	Chinese salt (*China uppu*)
2 tbsp.	–	Soya sauce (*Soyaa sauce*)
3 tbsp.	–	Tomato ketchup (*Thakali sauce*)
3 cups	–	Refined sunflower oil for frying (*Poripathuku ennai*)
Salt (*Uppu*)	–	To taste

Method:

1. Wash the cauliflower well and cut into large size florets
2. Soak the florets in salted hot water for 10 mins to remove any worms
3. Make a smooth thick batter of maida, corn flour,1 tbsp. of ginger garlic paste, red chili powder, salt and water
4. Heat oil in a frying pan. Dip the florets in the batter and deep fry till golden brown. Drain the oil on an oil absorbent paper
5. In another pan, heat 2 tbsp. oil
6. Add garlic, 1 tbsp. of ginger garlic paste, dry red chilies and green chilies
7. Stir fry for a minute. Add capsicum cubes and salt

8. Add spring onions
9. Add chinese salt, soya and tomato sauce. Mix well
10. Just before serving, add the fried florets into the gravy and mix well.
11. Garnish with finely chopped spring onions. Serve hot

Tip: To remove the strong smell of onions or non-vegetarian food from fingers and cutlery, wash them with warm water and lemon

Sunday Special – Tea Time Snacks and Treats

"Her children arise up, and call her Blessed.."

(Proverbs 31:28)

I loved writing out this section of recipes for you as they are so much fun. Each recipe is different not only in terms of ingredients and method used to prepare them but also in terms of the techniques used. But more so, because it reminded me of my childhood home and my mother who made every Sunday evening teatime a much awaited time with different kinds of yummy snacks and treats. When I grew older and left home for college to the hostel, she would pack snacks like *Diamond cuts, Omapodi* and *Doughnuts* in large airtight tins to last an entire semester. I have dedicated this section with a heart full of love to her.

On a Sunday, we all stay together at home to relax and eat hot food on a plate at the dining table with our families. So, I hope this section will help you make every Sunday evening special for your family too, with tasty teatime snacks and treats after a good afternoon nap. I hope they will also help you especially when you are planning a birthday party or after-school evening snacks for your kids. The recipes can also be used to prepare special treats for church picnics, Harvest festival sales or Sunday school outings. They are bound to be a big hit with everybody especially the kids.

Bajji's are the ideal snack to eat along with a cup of hot tea on a rainy day watching and listening to a drizzle. Pass around *Diamond cuts* and *Doughnuts* on a tour with friends or an excursion in the bus/train. For a tea party with girlfriends, serve *Croquettes* and *Raised doughnuts* along with fresh lemonade. Serve *Samosas, Spring rolls,* and *Patties* for a theme party or a baby shower or take them with you while visiting family friends. And for your relatives, aunts and uncles visiting you, nothing like *Masala vadai* served with freshly ground coconut chutney on a banana leaf. *Oma Podi* is a fried savoury dish that resembles vermicelli but is made with Bengal gram flour.

It can be eaten as it is or else crumbled into 'sev' and served over chaat dishes like sev puri, dahi puri, bhel puri and even pani puri.

Snacks are high calorie food items as they are deep fried in oil. Remember to drain as much oil as you can on absorbent paper before serving. Ketchups, sauces and chutneys can be served with them. Enjoy your Sunday!

Types of Snacks

All of us love snacking, especially kids. Though bakeries and food stores offer a large variety of packed snacks, making them at home is always a better option. One of the things I enjoy doing is watching the rain while eating samosas and sipping hot tea. It can warm you up and brighten up your spirit however gloomy and wet the weather is outside.

Types of Sweets

In South India, sweets are served as both starters and at the end of the meal. Festivals and weddings are incomplete with sweets. There are both wet sweets like *Halwa, Payasam* and *Basundi* etc and dry sweets like *kadala Mittai, Diamond cuts and Sangu seedai*. Some sweets like *Halwa* and *Payasam* taste awesome both when hot and when cold! Unique.

A lot of sweets are milk based like *Rasagollas* and *Pal Gova*. They are flavoured with almonds, cashewnuts and pistachios and decorated with silver leaf. Making sweets is a painstaking task but it is definitely worth the effort. While visiting a friend's home, the traditional gift to take is a box of assorted milk sweets and fruits.

Sugar Syrup String Consistency

While making sweets, sugar is made into syrup and sweets are soaked in it. Different sweets require different a different consistency of the sugar syrup and from Gulab Jamun to Kadala mittai, the success of a sweet depends on the consistency of the sugar syrup.

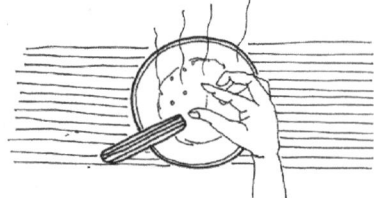

To do this, dip a wooden spatula in the boiling syrup and lift out. Allow cooling for a few seconds, as the syrup will be very hot. Now touch the syrup with your forefinger and then touch your thumb and forefinger together and pull them gently apart. A sugar syrup string will form between your fingers like 1-string or 2-strings. Keep boiling the syrup and check frequently and quickly, till you reach the consistency called for in the recipe for the sweet.

Given Below are the Different Stages for Consistency Check

Name	Sweets
Thin syrup	Juice
Sticky syrup	Gulab Jamun
½ string	Jaangari, Jalebi, Gulgul, Diamond cuts
1 string	Kaju katli, Badushah, Mysore pak, Badam barfi
2 string	Cashew burfi, Boondi, Ladoo, Mohanthal
3 string	Dhal burfi
Gathering consistency	–
Soft ball consistency	Fudge, Adirasam, Pori urundai
Firm ball consistency	Marshmallows
Hard ball consistency	Kadala mittai, toffees
Soft crack	Butterscotch
Hard crack	Glazed fruit
Golden brown caramel	Praline, Nougatines, Tirunelveli Halwa

Types of Savouries

Savoury snacks are perfect for teatime like *Muruku, Karachev, Thattai* etc., Savoury snacks are the best for bachelor parties and movie nights at home. Every kitchen will definitely have a squeezing press with different plates to make different types of snacks like *Om podi, Ribbon pakoda* etc.

41. Bread Bajji

Ingredients:

6	–	Bread slices (*Rotti thundugal*)
3 cups	–	Bengal gram flour (*Kadala mavu*)
1 cup	–	Rice flour (*Arasi mavu*)
1 cup	–	Roasted Bengal gram flour (*Pottu kadala mavu*)
¼ tsp.	–	Turmeric powder (*Manjal podi*)
1-½ tbsp.	–	Red chili powder (*Milagai podi*)
A pinch	–	Baking soda (*Aapa soda*)
2 sprigs	–	Curry leaves (*Karuvapaellai*), chopped finely
1 tsp.	–	Salt (*Uppu*)
3 cups	–	Refined sunflower oil for frying (*Poripathuku ennai*)

Method:

1. Cut the bread slices diagonally into 2 triangles or into 4 squares. There is no need to remove the edges
2. Mix all the other ingredients with water to make a thick batter of dipping consistency
3. Dip the bread slices in the batter
4. Deep fry in hot oil till golden brown
5. Drain the oil on absorbent paper or in a wired bowl.
6. Serve hot with tomato ketchup

Tip: The same recipe for bread bajji can be used to make different varieties of bajji's like *Egg bajji* using boiled egg halves, *Molaga bajji* using Ooty green chillies (stuffed or plain), *Potato bajji* and *Onion bajji* with thin slices of potatoes and onions, *Podalangai bajji* using snake gourd cored and cut into thin rings, *Keerai bajji* by dipping spinach leaves in the batter etc.,

42. Oma Podi

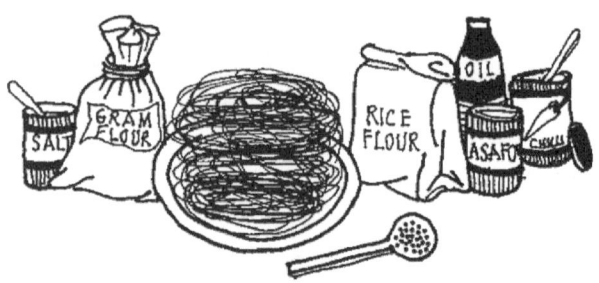

Ingredients:

1 cup	–	Bengal gram flour (*Kadala mavu*)
1 cup	–	Rice flour (*Arasi mavu*)
1 tbsp.	–	Carom seeds (*Omam*)
1 tbsp.	–	White butter (*Vennai*)
1 tbsp.	–	Red chili powder (*Milagai podi*)
¼ tsp.	–	Asafoetida (*Perungayam*)
To taste	–	Salt (*Uppu*)
3 cups	–	Refined sunflower oil for frying (*Poripathuku ennai*)

Method:

1. Soak carom seeds in ½ cup hot water for 10 minutes. Grind in the mixer
2. Strain the seeds and keep the carom flavoured water aside
3. Grease your palm with a little oil and mix all the other ingredients with the carom flavoured water to make a soft dough
4. Heat oil for frying
5. Put the dough in a greased *Omapodi mould* and squeeze directly into the hot oil

6. Turn over and cook till the bubbling stops
7. Drain on oil absorbent paper and store in an airtight container when cool

Tip: To make the oma podi crisper, add 1 tsp. of maida to the ingredients. For additional flavor, instead of asafoetida, grind 5 pods of garlic with the omam and water. Strain and use the water to make the dough

43. Diamond Cuts – Sweet and Karam

Sweet Diamond Cuts

Ingredients:

1 cup	–	Flour (*Maida mavu*)
¼ cup	–	Boiled milk (*Kothikavaitha Paal*)
¼ cup	–	Unsalted Butter (*Vennai*)
¼ cup	–	Sugar (*Sarkarai*)
¼ cup	–	Water
A pinch	–	Salt (*Uppu*)
3 cups	–	Refined sunflower oil for frying (*Poripathuku ennai*)

Method:
1. In a deep bowl rub butter into the flour to resemble breadcrumbs
2. Add milk and knead into a soft dough
3. Roll out the dough like a thin chapatti on a board

4. Use a cutter and cut criss-cross to get diamond shapes

5. Heat oil in a wok
6. Deep fry the diamond cuts in hot oil
7. Prepare sugar syrup by heating water with sugar until the sugar dissolves completely
8. Check for ½ string consistency of sugar syrup. Remove from heat
9. Dip the fried diamond cuts in the hot syrup and mix well to coat each diamond cut with sugar syrup
10. When it cools, the sugar will crystallise on the diamond cuts

Karam Diamond Cuts

Ingredients:

1 cup	–	Flour (*Maida mavu*)
¼ cup	–	Boiled milk (*Kothikavaitha Paal*)
¼ cup	–	Unsalted Butter (*Vennai*)
1 tsp.	–	Pepper powder (*Milagu thul*)
1 tsp.	–	Red chili powder (*Milagai podi*)
A pinch	–	Salt (*Uppu*)
3 cups	–	Refined sunflower oil for frying (*Poripathuku ennai*)

Method:

1. In a deep bowl rub butter into the Flour to resemble breadcrumbs
2. Add milk and knead into a soft dough
3. Roll out the dough like a thin chapatti on a board
4. Use a cutter and cut crisscross to get diamond shapes

5. Heat oil in a wok
6. Deep fry the karam diamond cuts in hot oil

Tip: To make clean sugar syrup, boil the sugar in an equal quanitity of water. Add a little milk mixed with water. After some time, any dirt in the sugar will rise to the top. Remove it with a spoon and continue boiling the clean sugar syrup to the desired consistency.

44. Doughnuts

Ingredients:

1 cup	–	Flour (*Maida mavu*)
1	–	Eggs (*Muttai*)
A pinch	–	Baking Soda (*Aapa soda*)
¼ cup	–	Powdered sugar (*Poditha sarkarai*)
2 tbsp.	–	Butter (*Vennai*)
½ tsp.	–	Vanilla Esssence (*Vanilla saarai*)
3 cups	–	Refined sunflower oil for frying (*Poripathuku ennai*)

Method:
1. Sift flour and baking soda together
2. In a deep bowl, rub butter into the Flour and baking soda till it resembles bread crumbs
3. Beat the eggs well with sugar and vanilla essence
4. Add to the Flour and knead into a stiff dough. Do not add water

as it will become soggy.
5. Roll out on a floured board to ⅛" thickness. Dust in Flour if necessary
6. Use a doughnut cutter to cut the classic round doughnut shape or else use different cookie cutters to cut shapes like stars, hearts, flowers etc

7. Heat oil for frying
8. Deep fry the doughnuts in hot oil
9. Drain on oil absorbent paper
10. When cool, dip the doughnuts in chocolate sauce or dust icing sugar on top

Tips:

* While cutting shapes for the doughnuts dip the cookie cutter in flour before cutting. This will prevent the cookie cutter from sticking and ensure a clean cut

* After cutting different shapes, place the doughnuts on a floured plate before frying. This will prevent the doughnuts from sticking to the plate

45. Samosa

Ingredients:

½ cup	−	Flour (*Maida mavu*)
½ cup	−	Wheat flour (*Gothumai mavu*)
1 tbsp.	−	Vanaspati ghee (*Dalda*) Filling:
2	−	Potatoes (*Urulaikkilangu*)
1	−	Onions (*Vengayam*), finely chopped
1	−	Green chilies (*Pachai milagai*), finely chopped
¼ tsp.	−	Turmeric powder (*Manjal podi*)
1 tbsp.	−	Coriander powder (*Malli podi*)
1 tbsp.	−	Red chili powder (*Milagai podi*)
1 tsp.	−	Chaat masala (*Chaat masala podi*), (optional)
8	−	Cashewnuts (*Mundiri*), halved
8	−	Raisins (*Ularnta thirachai*)
1 sprig	−	Curry leaves (*Karuvapaellai*), finely chopped
¼ cup	−	Coriander leaves (*Kothamali elai*), finely chopped
½ tsp.	−	Mustard (*Kadugu*)
½ tsp.	−	Cumin seeds (*Seeragam*)
To taste	−	Salt (*Uppu*)
1 tbsp.	−	Ghee (*Nei*)
3 cups	−	Refined sunflower oil for frying (*Poripathuku ennai*)

Method:

1. Boil the potatoes. Peel the skin and mash well
2. Heat 2 tbsp. oil in a wok
3. Season with mustard and cumin seeds
4. Saute onions
5. Add green chilies and curry leaves
6. Add turmeric powder, coriander and red chili powder
7. Add chaat masala and salt

8. Add the mashed potatoes and mix well
9. Cover and cook under a lid for 2 minutes
10. Add coriander leaves
11. Fry cashewnuts and raisins in 1 tbsp. of ghee.
12. Add this to the potato mix. Now the filling is ready
13. Mix together flour and wheat flour with vanaspati ghee to resemble bread crumbs
14. Add cold water to make a soft dough. Keep aside for ½ hour
15. Make balls and roll out like pooris
16. Cut into 2 as shown in the picture

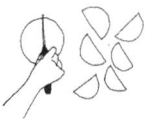

17. Roll each half into a cone

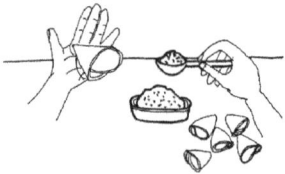

18. Put the filling inside and seal the top with a little water

19. Deep fry in hot oil till golden brown. Drain on oil absorbent paper and serve hot with ketchup.

Variations of the Samosa fold

a) Simple triangular fold

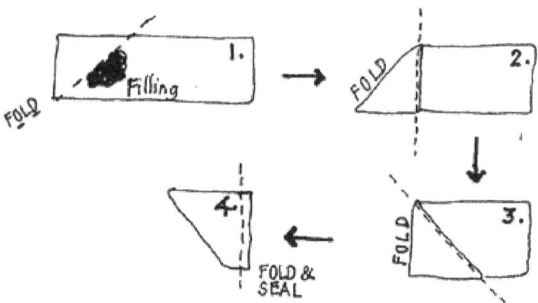

b) Wanton fold

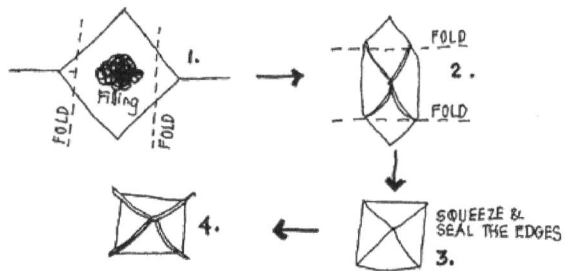

c) Praying hands fold

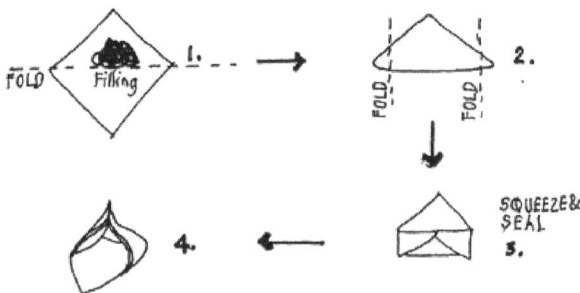

Tip: Fried food should never be kept covered as it will lose its crispness and become soggy

46. Chicken Croquettes

Ingredients:

10	–	Bread slices (*Rotti thundugal*)
1 cup	–	Boneless chicken mince (*Kozhi kothu kari*)
1	–	Potatoes (*Urulaikkilangu*)
1	–	Onions (*Vengayam*), finely chopped
½	–	Tomatoes (*Thakali*)
1 tbsp.	–	Ginger garlic paste (*Inji poondu viluthu*)
½ tsp.	–	Turmeric powder (*Manjal podi*)
1 tsp.	–	Coriander powder (*Malli podi*)
1 tsp.	–	Red chili powder (*Milagai podi*)
¼ tsp.	–	Garam masala (*Garam masala podi*)
1 tsp.	–	Cumin seeds (*Seeragam*)
½ cup	–	Coriander leaves (*Kothamali elai*)
To taste	–	Salt (*Uppu*)
2 tbsp.	–	Gingelly oil (*Nalla ennai*)
3 cups	–	Refined sunflower oil for frying (*Poripathuku ennai*)

Method:

1. Steam cook the chicken in the pressure cooker for 2 whistles.
2. When cook, shred the chicken or mince it in the mixer
3. Boil the potato well. Remove the skin and mash well
4. In a wok, heat 2 tbsp. oil
5. Add cumin seeds

6. Saute onions
7. Add ginger garlic paste
8. Add the shredded chicken
9. Add turmeric, coriander and red chili powder and garam masala
10. Add tomato and salt
11. Add the mashed potato
12. Add coriander leaves and remove from heat. This is the filling
13. To prepare the croquette, take a little water in a shallow bowl. Dip each slice of bread in the water for just a second. Remove and place the slice between both palms and squeeze out the water.
14. Take a little filling and put it in the middle. Roll up the bread in your hand tightly taking care to seal it well. Shape into an oblong cutlet shape and keep aside. Do this one at a time.
15. Deep fry in hot oil. Serve hot with tomato or chilly ketchup

Tip: Bread can be preserved longer if stored in the original wrapping and kept in the lower shelf of the refrigerator

47. Spring Roll

Ingredients:
Pancake:

1 cup	–	Flour (*Maida mavu*)
½ cup	–	Corn flour (*Solla mavu*)

1	–	Eggs (*Muttai*)
2 tsp.	–	Gingelly oil (*Nalla ennai*)
As required	–	Water
A pinch	–	Salt (*Uppu*) Filling:
1	–	Onions (*Vengayam*), finely chopped
½	–	Cabbage (*Muttai ghoz*), finely chopped
2	–	Grated carrot (*Thuruviya manjal mulangi*),
2 tbsp.	–	Pepper powder (*Milagu thul*)
A pinch	–	Chinese salt (*China uppu*)
1 tsp.	–	Soya sauce (*Soya sauce*)
5	–	Green chilies (*Pachai milagai*), finely chopped
3 cups	–	Refined sunflower oil for frying (*Poripathuku ennai*)
½ cup	–	Gingelly oil (*Nalla ennai*), for sautéing vegetables and making the spring roll sheets
To taste	–	Salt (*Uppu*)
2 tbsp.	–	Flour (*Maida mavu*), for sealing the spring roll sheets

Method:

1. Mix together all the ingredients for the pancake with a little water to get a semi thick batter. Keep aside for 1 hour
2. To make the spring roll sheet, pour out a ladle full of batter on a hot tava like a pancake or dosai (either square shape or round). Smear oil all around for it to cook
3. Remove and keep aside

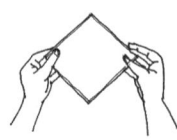

4. In a wok, heat 2 tbsp. oil

5. Saute onions
6. Add green chilies
7. Add cabbage and carrots
8. Add pepper and salt
9. Cover and cook for a 5 minutes
10. Add soya sauce and ajinomoto
11. The filling is ready.
12. Now put a little filling in the lower end of each spring roll sheet

13. Fold the lower end to secure the filling

14. Fold the side ends of the sheet like an envelope

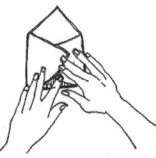

15. Now start rolling up from below, as shown in the figure

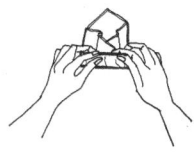

16. Make a paste of flour and water and use this to seal the edges so that the filling does not spill out

17. Deep fry the rolls in hot oil.

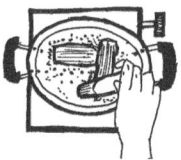

18. Drain on oil absorbent paper
19. Serve the spring rolls hot with tomato ketchup

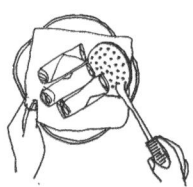

Tip: Always store cumin seeds, garam masala and other masalas in a cool, dark place as they tend to lose their flavor in light.

48. Patties

Ingredients:

Base:

2 cups	–	Flour (*Maida mavu*)
2 tbsp.	–	Cold Butter (*Vennai*)
½ tsp.	–	Salt (*Uppu*)
As required	–	Cold Water, for binding

Filling:

1 cup	–	Minced chicken (*Kozhi kothu kari*)
1 tsp.	–	Cumin seeds (*Seeragam*)
1	–	Onions (*Vengayam*), finely chopped
½	–	Capsicum (*Kudai milagai*), finely chopped
1 tbsp.	–	Ginger garlic paste (*Inji poondu viluthu*)
4 tsp.	–	Turmeric powder (*Manjal podi*)
1 tsp.	–	Coriander powder (*Malli podi*)
½ tsp.	–	Red chili powder (*Milagai podi*)
¼ tsp.	–	Garam Masala (*Garam masala podi*)
½ cup	–	Coriander leaves (*Kothamali elai*), finely chopped
To taste	–	Salt (*Uppu*)
2 tbsp.	–	Gingelly oil (*Nalla ennai*)
3 cups	–	Refined sunflower oil for frying (*Poripathuku ennai*)

Method:

1. Heat 2 tbsp. oil in a wok
2. Add cumin seeds
3. Saute onions and capsicum
4. When the onions turn transparent, add ginger garlic paste
5. Add minced chicken
6. Add ¼ cup coriander leaves
7. Add turmeric powder, coriander powder, red chili powder
8. Add garam masala and salt

9. Cover and cook for 10 minutes
10. Add ¼ cup coriander leaves. This is the filling for the patties
11. Rub cold butter into the flour and salt till it resembles bread crumbs
12. Sprinkle cold water and knead into a soft dough
13. Divide into large balls
14. Roll out each ball into a circle on a floured board

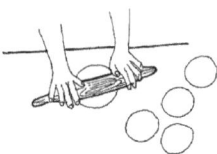

15. Put 2 tbsp. full of filling in the middle and fold the circles

16. Seal the edges with water

17. Curl the edges to give a decorative look or use a patty cutter to give the edge a serrated effect

18. Deep fry in hot oil. Drain the oil in absorbent paper. Serve hot with chutney or ketchup

Tips:
* Do not add too much filling or else it will spill out
* The same recipe can be used with different fillings like minced mutton or a sweet mixture of coconut and jaggery

49. Masala Vadai

Ingredients:

1 cup	–	Bengal gram (*Kadala parupu*)
1	–	Onions (*Vengayam*), finely chopped
½ tsp.	–	Asafoetida (*Perungayam*)
2	–	Green chilies (*Pachai milagai*), finely chopped
2 sprigs	–	Curry leaves (*Karuvapaellai*), finely chopped
3 cups	–	Refined sunflower oil for frying (*Poripathuku ennai*)

Method:
1. Soak the Bengal gram for 4 hours. Drain the water
2. Keep ¼ cup aside as it is. Grind the remaining ¾ cup to a coarse paste
3. Add onions, asafoetida, green chilies, curry leaves and salt. Grind lightly using the whisk mode to combine everything
4. Make lime size balls. Flatten out to form vadais

5. Deep fry in hot oil till golden brown. Lower the flame so that the insides also get cooked well
6. Serve hot with ketchup or chutney

Tip: While it is not at all advisable to re-use fried oil, if there is an unavoidable situation where it has to be used, strain the oil before using it again to remove all the fried bits and pieces

50. Raised Doughnuts

Ingredients:

2 cups	–	Flour (*Maida mavu*)
2 tbsp.	–	Dry yeast (*Ularnta yeast*)
½ cup	–	Sugar (*Sarkarai*)
1 tsp.	–	Salt (*Uppu*)
25 g	–	Unsalted butter (*Vennai*)
25 g	–	Milk powder (*Paal podi*)
1	–	Eggs (*Muttai*)
1 tsp.	–	Bread improver
1 cup	–	Chocolate sauce
¼ cup	–	Flour (*Maida mavu*) for dusting
3 cups	–	Oil for frying (*Poripathuku ennai*)

Method:

1. Mix together flour, dry yeast, salt, sugar, bread improver and milk powder
2. Add an egg

3. Add butter
4. Add 1 cup of water and knead into a dough
5. Spread flour onto a smooth flat surface. Knead the dough. Roll out the dough. Now fold it. Knead again. Roll out the dough. Now fold again. This will enable the dough to be filled with air pockets
6. Keep aside for 5 hours under a wet muslin cloth, so that it doubles in size
7. Now roll out the dough to ½ "thickness

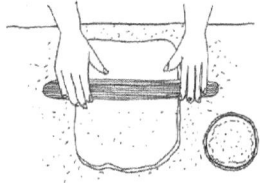

8. Use a doughnut cutter, cut out doughnuts. Dip the cutter in flour every time before cutting to get a neat cut

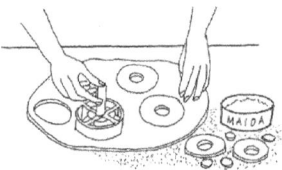

9. Place the doughnuts under a wet muslin cloth. Wait for 1 hour so that it again doubles in size
10. Heat oil in a deep bottom wok. Deep fry the doughnuts in hot oil till golden brown

11. Drain the oil and allow to cool.

12. Dip the doughnuts in chocolate sauce when cool. Shake it a little to remove excess sauce
13. Optional: Sprinkle icing sugar, or sprinkles on top

Chocolate Sauce

Ingredients:

100 g	–	Icing sugar
2 tbsp.	–	Cocoa powder (*Cocoa thul*)
1 tbsp.	–	Unsalted butter (*Vennai*)
½ cup	–	Water

Method:
1. Put all the above ingredients in a sauce pan and heat on simmer till a thick sauce is formed

Tip: Chocolates, coffee powder, nuts and dried fruits can be preserved for a longer period by storing them in the refrigerator. Keep chocolate bars always wrapped tightly in foil. Never leave chocolate bars open as they will absorb all the other flavours in the refrigerator and lose their flavour.

Everyday Curries

A gracious woman retaineth honour...

(Proverbs 11:16)

Everyday cooking can transform from a mandane must-do chore to something exciting and extraordinary by serving a completely new curry on the table every day. A curry is a must-be-there-on-the-table dish and a well-known part of Indian cuisine, called '***Kozhambu***' in Tamil. It is the accompaniment dish to rice, chapatti and tiffin items such as vadai etc., It is prepared with vegetables or meat in a tomato and onion base. Spices and herbs impart flavour, heat and pungency to the curry; very, very, very rarely is a curry sweet (***Navaratna curry***). Lentils such as red gram, Bengal gram or green gram thicken the curry. Coconut milk and cashew paste are used sometimes to add richness to the curry. Different types of curries include Dhal, Sambar, Stew, Kurma, Non-vegetarian gravy, Vindaloo, Tikka masala etc.,

Sambar rules over all the other curries as the queen. This is because it is highly nutritious and hence is served alongside almost all the south indian breakfast dishes such as idly, dosai, pngal, at lunch and dinner with steamed rice as well as at tea time with vadai. So, its presence on the dining table is definite, the whole daylong. Sambar is made with a base vegetable(s), red gram, sambar powder and tamarind. Sambar is my all time favourite curry and the one dish I am completely amazed by. This is because of its versatality and ability to have a zillion variations in taste by changing just one ingredient i.e., the base vegetable. You can make it with exclusively one vegetable or a combination of vegetables. That means so many different tasting sambars can be made by usin'g the same recipe!

Some of the varieties of sambar are Drumstick Sambar, Carrot, Beans & Radish Sambar, Shallots (***Sambar vengayam***) Sambar, Brinjal Sambar, Ladies Finger Sambar, Keerai Sambar, Peerkangai Sambar, Raw Mango sambar and so on. Hence a number of permutations and combinations are possible with this dish. My personal favourite is the Pumpkin sambar.

Sambar powder is the ingredient that makes sambar unique from all other curries. It is like a spice powder that enhances the flavour of the sambar.

Every household in south india has an unshared secret recipe for their own home's sambar powder. It is essentially made by grinding dry roasted indian spices such as mustard, peppercorns, dry red chilies, fenugreek, coriander seeds, Bengal gram etc.,

Types of Lentils

Lentils are extremely healthy and provide you with essential nutrients. Soaking lentils in water for a few hours softens them. Once they are boiled and mashed, they can be added to a curry like sambar or dhal. Lentils like chickpeas require a minimum of 4 hours of soaking and take a longer time to soften and cook.

Split - Red gram (Thoovaram parupu)	Bengal gram (kadalai parupu)	Split - Black gram (Ullutham parupu)
Split - Green gram (Pasi parupu)	Split - Red lentil (Masoor parupu)	Whole - Black gram (Ullutham parupu)
Whole - Green gram (Pasi parupu)	Black eyed peas (Karamani)	Red kidney beans (Rajma)
White Chickpeas (Vellai konda kadalai)	Soya beans (Soya)	Brown Chickpeas (Karuppu konda kadalai)

Types of Spices

At the heart of all Indian cooking are the spices, each having its own unique flavour and aromatic characteristic. They also have medicinal value and in my kitchen I add cumin seeds to every curry including sambar as they aid in digestion.

Cinnamon	Cloves	Cardamom
Star anise	Fennel	Cumin
Sesame seeds	Black peppercorns	Fenugreek
Bay leaf	Mustard	Nutmeg
Coriander seeds	Dry red chilly (long)	Dry red chilly (round)

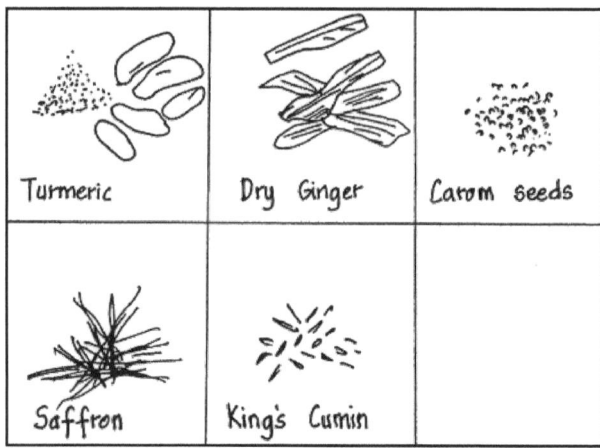

In days of old, spices like dry red chilly, peppercorns etc used to be ground to a powder in a mortar and pestle or to a paste in the traditional 'Ammi' and then added to the curry. But today all the ground masalas are readily available in a grocery store or supermarket and can be added directly from a packet.

Masala Milk for Good Health

Ingredients:

1 cup	–	Warm milk (*Kothikavaitha Paal*)
1 tsp.	–	Sugar (*Sarkarai*)
¼ tsp.	–	Turmeric powder (*Manjal podi*)
½ tsp.	–	Pepper powder (*Milagu thul*)

Method:

1. Mix all the above ingredients together. Having a glass of this masala milk every night keeps you healthy.

Types of Herbs

Herbs like coriander, curry leaves and mint are extensively used in South Indian cooking in curries and poriyals. They can also be used to prepare tasty chutneys like Mint chutney and Coriander chutney. Curry leaves can be sun dried and ground with other ingredients to a powder (*Karuvapillai podi*), which can be mixed in rice and eaten. Spices like oregano are sprinkled over Pizza.

51. Dhal

Ingredients:

1/3 cup	–	Red gram (*Thoovaram parupu*)
1	–	Onions (*Vengayam*), finely chopped
1	–	Tomatoes (*Thakali*), finely chopped
3	–	Green chilies (*Pachai milagai*), finely chopped
12	–	Garlic (*Poondu*)
¼ tsp.	–	Asafoetida (*Perungayam*)
1 tsp.	–	Mustard (*Kadugu*)
1 tsp.	–	Black gram (*Ullutham parupu*)
1 tsp.	–	Cumin seeds (*Seeragam*)
3	–	Dry red chilly (*Kanja milagai*)
2 sprigs	–	Curry leaves (*Karuvapaellai*), finely chopped
½ cup	–	Coriander leaves (*Kothamali elai*), finely chopped
½ tsp.	–	Turmeric Powder (*Manjal podi*)
½ tsp.	–	Red chili powder (*Milagai podi*)
2 tbsp.	–	Grated Coconut (*Thuruviya thengai*)
2 tbsp.	–	Gingelly Oil (*Nalla ennai*)
1 tbsp.	–	Ghee (*Nei*)
To taste	–	Salt (*Uppu*)

Method:
1. Soak red gram for 2 hours or more in 2 cups of water
2. Add tomato, green chilies, asafoetida, 1 tsp. salt, 1 tbsp. gingelly oil and garlic to the red gram and water. Pressure cook this for 3 whistles
3. In a wok, heat 1 tbsp. oil and 1 tbsp. ghee
4. Season the oil with mustard
5. When the mustard splutters, add black gram and cumin
6. Add dry red chili broken into two
7. Add onions and saute well
8. Add half the quantity of curry leaves and coriander leaves
9. Simmer the flame and add turmeric powder and red chili powder
10. Add the boiled red gram and mix well. Let it come to a boil
11. Add the remaining curry leaves and coriander leaves
12. Add grated coconut and let it cook for a minute. Remove from the fire and serve hot with rice and potato fry

Tip: Always store eggs in the refrigerator. Cold eggs separate better and clearer as yolks and whites. While storing eggs, place them in the egg tray with their pointed end facing down

52. Sambar

Ingredients:
½ cup	–	Red gram *(Thoovaram parupu)*
¼ kg	–	Pumpkin *(Pusanikai)*, skinned and cubed

1	–	Onions (*Vengayam*), finely chopped
1	–	Tomatoes (*Thakali*), finely chopped
¼ tsp.	–	Asafoetida (*Perungayam*)
1 tsp.	–	Mustard (*Kadugu*)
1 tsp.	–	Black gram (*Ullutham parupu*)
1 tsp.	–	Cumin seeds (*Seeragam*)
2	–	Dry red chilies (kanja milagai), broken into two
½ tsp.	–	Turmeric powder (*Manjal podi*)
1 tsp.	–	Coriander powder (*Malli podi*)
½ tsp.	–	Red chili powder (*Milagai podi*)
2 tbsp.	–	Sambar powder (*Sambar podi*)
1 lime size	–	Tamarind (*Puli*)
½" piece	–	Jaggery (*Vellam*)
2 sprigs	–	Curry leaves (*Karuvapaellai*), finely chopped
½ cup	–	Coriander leaves (*Kothamali elai*), finely chopped
To taste	–	Salt (*Uppu*)
1 tbsp.	–	Ghee (*Nei*)
1 tbsp. + 1 tbsp	–	Gingelly oil (*Nalla ennai*)

Method:

1. Pressure cook red gram with water, 1 tbsp. oil, asafetida, pumpkin cubes and 1 tsp. salt for 3 whistles
2. Remove and allow to cool. When it has cooled, mash the boiled red gram till it softens to a smooth paste
3. Heat 1 tbsp. oil and 1 tbsp. ghee in a wok
4. Season with mustard, urad dhal and Cumin seeds
5. Add red dry chilies
6. Saute onions
7. Add 1 sprig of curry leaves and ¼ cup of coriander leaves finely chopped
8. Add turmeric powder, coriander powder and red chili powder
9. Add sambar powder

10. Add tomatoes and salt
11. When the tomatoes soften, add the boiled red gram and pumpkin. Mix well
12. When it starts bubbling, add tamarind extract
13. Add a piece of jaggery
14. Put off the stove and add 1 sprig of curry leaves and ¼ cup of coriander leaves finely chopped

Tip: If a curry turns out a little over-salted, toss in a couple of peeled potatoes into the curry. Remove them just before serving. The curry will taste just right!

53. Puli Kozhambu

Ingredients:

1	–	Onions (*Vengayam*), finely chopped
2	–	Drumsticks (*Murungakai*), chopped into pieces
2	–	Tomatoes (*Thakali*), pureed
¼ tsp.	–	Turmeric powder (*Manjal podi*)
2 tsp.	–	Coriander powder (*Malli podi*)
1 tsp.	–	Red chili powder (*Milagai podi*)
1 tsp.	–	Mustard (*Kadugu*)
1 tsp.	–	Black gram (*Ullutham parupu*)
1 tbsp.	–	Dried onions (*Vengaya Vatral*)
1 lime size	–	Tamarind (*Puli*)
½ cup	–	Coconut milk (*Thengai paal*), thick

½" piece	–	Jaggery (*Vellam*)
2 sprigs	–	Curry leaves (*Karuvapaellai*), finely chopped
3 tbsp.	–	Gingelly Oil (*Nalla ennai*)

Method:

1. Heat oil in a wok
2. Add mustard
3. When the mustard splutters, add black gram and slightly roast
4. Add onions and curry leaves
5. Add vengaya vatral
6. Toss in the drumstick pieces and fry lightly
7. Simmer and add turmeric powder, coriander powder and red chili powder. Mix well
8. Add the tomato puree and salt
9. Add 1 cup of water.
10. Cover and cook for 15 minutes until the drumsticks soften
11. Add tamarind extract made by dissolving the tamarind piece in 1-½ cups of hot water, Bring to a boil
12. Add jiggery
13. Add thick coconut milk.

Tip: When you want to add more water to the curry to dilute a curry, add only HOT water. Never add cold water as it will alter the taste of the curry

54. Channa Kozhambu

Ingredients:

1 cup	–	White chickpeas or Channa (*Vellai konda kadalai*)
2	–	Onions (*Vengayam*), finely chopped
3	–	Tomatoes (*Thakali*), pureed
2 tbsp.	–	Ginger garlic paste (*Inji poondu viluthu*)
3	–	Green chilies (*Pachai milagai*), full, not chopped
½ tsp.	–	Asafoetida (*Perungayam*)
1" stick	–	Cinnamon (*Pattai*)
6	–	Cloves (*Krambu*)
1 tsp.	–	Cumin seeds (*Seeragam*)
½ tsp.	–	Turmeric powder (*Manjal podi*)
2 tsp.	–	Coriander powder (*Malli podi*)
1 tsp.	–	Red chili powder (*Milagai podi*)
2 tbsp.	–	Channa Masala
1 tbsp.	–	Tamarind paste (*Puli saaru*)
1 tbsp.	–	Date syrup (*Perichampazham saaru*)
1 small piece	–	Jaggery (*Vellam*)
½ cup	–	Coriander leaves (*Kothamali elai*), finely chopped
2 sprigs	–	Curry leaves (*Karuvapaellai*), finely chopped
3 tbsp.	–	Gingelly oil (*Nalla ennai*)
To taste	–	Salt (*Uppu*)

Method:

1. Soak chickpeas for 8 hours or overnight in 3 cups of water
2. Pressure cook chickpeas with water, asafoetida and 1 tsp. salt for 8 whistles so that it softens
3. In a wok, heat oil
4. Add cloves and cinnamon
5. Add cumin seeds
6. Add onions and saute till slightly brown
7. Chop the two ends of green chilies and add
8. Add curry leaves and ¼ cup coriander leaves

9. Simmer and add ginger garlic paste
10. Add turmeric powder, coriander powder and red chili powder
11. Add channa masala
12. Add tomato puree and salt
13. When the oil separates add the cooked chickpeas with the water. Let it boil well
14. Add tamarind paste
15. Add date syrup
16. Add jaggery
17. Add coriander leaves
18. Serve hot with Baturas or chapatis

Tip: Green chillies can be preserved for a longer time by removing the stalks. Store them in a plastic container in the refrigerator

55. Keerai Kozhambu

Ingredients:

½ cup	–	Green gram (*Pasi parupu*)
1 bunch	–	Greens (*Ara keerai or Siru keerai*)
1	–	Onions (*Vengayam*), finely chopped
1	–	Tomatoes (*Thakali*), finely chopped
3	–	Green chilies (*Pachai milagai*), slit
8	–	Garlic (*Poondu*)
½ tsp.	–	Asafoetida (*Perungayam*)
½ tsp.	–	Turmeric powder (*Manjal podi*)
2 tsp.	–	Sambar powder (*Sambar podi*)

1 tsp.	–	Mustard (*Kadugu*)
1 tsp.	–	Black gram (*Ullutham parupu*)
1 tsp.	–	Cumin seeds (*Seeragam*)
3	–	Dry red chilies (kanja milagai), broken into 2
1 tsp.	–	Tamarind paste (*Puli saaru*)
2 tbsp.	–	Grated coconut (*Thuruviya thengai*)
2 sprigs	–	Curry leaves (*Karuvapaellai*), finely chopped
½ cup	–	Coriander leaves (*Kothamali elai*), finely chopped
1 tbsp.	–	Ghee (*Nei*)
2 tbsp.	–	Gingelly oil (*Nalla ennai*)
To taste	–	Salt (*Uppu*)

Method:

1. Wash the greens well, under running water. Remove the leaves from the stalk and chop finely. You can use any variety of greens with small leaves
2. Pressure cook the greens with green gram, 1 tbsp. oil, asafoetida, tomatoes, green chilies and garlic for 3 whistles
3. In a wok, heat 1 tbsp. oil and 1 tbsp. ghee
4. Season with mustard
5. When the mustard splutters, add black gram and dry red chilies
6. Add cumin seeds
7. Add onions
8. Add curry leaves and ¼ cup coriander leaves
9. Add turmeric powder, sambar powder and salt
10. Add the cooked green gram mixture
11. Add tamarind paste and let it boil
12. Grind grated coconut with water to a paste. Add this paste. When it boils, remove from heat
13. Serve hot with rice and valaka fry

Tip: Do not let any kozhambu boil too much after adding coconut paste or coconut milk. Remove from heat after one bubble to prevent curdling

56. Poondu Kozhambu

Ingredients:

15	–	Garlic (*Poondu*)
1	–	Onions (*Vengayam*), finely chopped
2	–	Tomatoes (*Thakali*), pureed
1 tbsp.	–	Tamarind paste (*Puli saaru*)
½ cup	–	Coconut milk (*Thengai paal*), thick
¼ tsp.	–	Turmeric powder (*Manjal podi*)
2 tsp.	–	Coriander powder (*Malli podi*)
1 tsp.	–	Red chili powder (*Milagai podi*)
2 sprigs	–	Curry leaves (*Karuvapaellai*), finely chopped
1 tsp.	–	Mustard (*Kadugu*)
1 tsp.	–	Black gram (*Ullutham parupu*)
½" piece	–	Jaggery (*Vellam*)
1 tbsp.	–	Dried onions (*Vengaya Vatral*)
3 tbsp.	–	Gingelly Oil (*Nalla ennai*)

Method:
1. Heat oil in a wok
2. Add mustard
3. When the mustard splutters, add black gram and slightly roast
4. Add onions and saute until it becomes transparent
5. Add dried onions and curry leaves finely chopped
6. Toss in the garlic pods and mix well
7. Simmer and add turmeric powder, coriander powder and red chili powder

8. After a minute add the tomato puree and salt
9. Add 1 cup of water
10. Cover and cook for 5 minutes until garlic softens and the oil separates
11. Dissolve the tamarind paste in 1-½ cups of hot water and add. Bring to a boil
12. Add jaggery
13. Add thick coconut milk. Do not cover after this stage
14. The Poondu Kozhambu is ready. It should not be served immediately but tastes best after a few hours or the next day with steamed rice, omlette and Applam

Tip: Garlic is well known for its medicinal properties for lowering cholesterol. So add plenty of garlic in curries such as dhal, rasam etc., This kozhambu can be served to a new mother

57. Rasam

Ingredients:

1 cup	–	Dhal water drained after pressure cooking dhal (*Parupu thani*)
		or
		Water drained after cooking rice (*Kanji thani*)
½ tsp.	–	Mustard (*Kadugu*)
1 tsp.	–	Cumin seeds (*Seeragam*)
¼ tsp.	–	Asafoetida (*Perungayam*)
3	–	Garlic (*Poondu*), crushed

1	–	Tomato (*Thakali*), crushed
2 tsp.	–	Pepper powder (*Milagu thul*)
1	–	Lime, juice (*Elumichai saaru*)
2 sprigs	–	Curry leaves (*Karuvapaellai*), finely chopped
½ cup	–	Coriander leaves (*Kothamali elai*), finely chopped
2 tbsp.	–	Gingelly oil (*Nalla ennai*)

Method:
1. Heat oil in a wok
2. Add mustard
3. Add cumin seeds
4. Add finely chopped curry leaves
5. Simmer and add asafetida
6. Add the dhal water, crushed tomatoes and garlic
7. Add pepper powder and salt
8. Add coriander leaves
9. Let it boil for 2–3 minutes
10. Remove from heat. The rasam is ready
11. Now, squeeze the juice of one lime into the rasam

Tip: Keep coriander leaves in an airtight plastic box with a paper napkin inside in the refrigerator. They will stay fresh for a long time

58. Pasi Parupu Kozhambu

Ingredients:

1/3 cup	–	Green gram (*Pasi parupu*)
1	–	Onions (*Vengayam*), finely chopped
1	–	Tomatoes (*Thakali*), finely chopped
3	–	Green chilies (*Pachai milagai*), finely chopped
12	–	Garlic (*Poondu*)
¼ tsp.	–	Asafoetida (*Perungayam*)
1 tsp.	–	Mustard (*Kadugu*)
1 tsp.	–	Black gram (*Ullutham parupu*)
1 tsp.	–	Cumin seeds (*Seeragam*)
3	–	Dry red chili (*Kanja milagai*), broken into two
2 sprigs	–	Curry leaves (*Karuvapaellai*), finely chopped
½ cup	–	Coriander leaves (*Kothamali elai*), finely chopped
½ tsp.	–	Turmeric Powder (*Manjal podi*)
½ tsp.	–	Red chili powder (*Milagai podi*)
2 tbsp.	–	Grated Coconut (*Thuruviya thengai*)
2 tbsp.	–	Gingelly Oil (*Nalla ennai*)
1 tbsp.	–	Ghee (*Nei*)
To taste	–	Salt (*Uppu*)

Method:

1. Pressure cook green gram with tomato, green chilies, asafoetida, 1 tsp. salt, 1 tbsp. gingelly oil, garlic and water for 3 whistles
2. In a wok, heat 1 tbsp. oil and 1 tbsp. ghee
3. Season the oil with mustard seeds
4. When the mustard seeds splutter, add black gram and cumin seeds
5. Add dry red chilies broken into two
6. Add onions and saute well
7. Add half the quantity of curry leaves and coriander leaves
8. Simmer the flame and add turmeric powder and red chili powder

9. Add the cooked green gram and mix well. Let it come to a boil. Check for salt and add more if necessary
10. Add the remaining curry leaves and coriander leaves
11. Add grated coconut and let it cook for a minute
12. Remove from the fire and serve hot with rice and potato fry

Tip: There is no need to pre-soak green gram as it cooks very fast. Dry roasting it for a few minutes before cooking brings out a nice flavour in the curry

59. Vendaka Kara Kozhambu

Ingredients:

1	–	Onions (***Vengayam***), finely chopped
6	–	Ladies fingers (***Vendaka***), cut into 3 pieces each
2	–	Tomatoes (***Thakali***), pureed
¼ tsp.	–	Turmeric powder (***Manjal podi***)
2 tsp.	–	Coriander powder (***Malli podi***)
1 tsp.	–	Red chili powder (***Milagai podi***)
1 tbsp.	–	Pepper corns (***Milagu***)
2 sprigs	–	Curry leaves (***Karuvapaellai***), finely chopped
1 tsp.	–	Mustard (***Kadugu***)
1 tsp.	–	Black gram (***Ullutham parupu***)
1 tbsp.	–	Dried onions (***Vengaya Vatral***)

½" piece	–	Jaggery (*Vellam*)
1 tbsp.	–	Tamarind paste (*Puli saaru*)
½ cup	–	Coconut milk (*Thengai paal*), thick
3 tbsp.	–	Gingelly Oil (*Nalla ennai*)

Method:

1. Dry fry ladies' finger pieces in a wok to remove all the moisture. Remove and keep aside
2. Heat oil in a wok
3. Add mustard
4. When the mustard splutters, add black gram and pepper corns
5. Saute onions until it becomes transparent
6. Add dried onions and curry leaves finely chopped
7. Toss in the ladies' finger pieces and mix well
8. Simmer and add turmeric powder, coriander powder and red chili powder
9. After a minute add the tomato puree and salt
10. Cover and cook for 5 minutes until the ladies finger pieces cook and the oil separates
11. Dissolve the tamarind paste in 1-½ cups of hot water. Bring to a boil
12. Add a piece of jaggery
13. Add thick coconut milk. Do not cover after this stage
14. Serve with steamed rice and curds

Tip: Finely chop both coriander and curry leaves before adding to any curry or poriyal. This ensures it is not discarded as a waste in the corner of the plate but rather is consumed along with the food

60. Muttai Kozhambu

Ingredients:

3	–	Eggs (*Muttai*)
2	–	Onions (*Vengayam*), finely chopped
3	–	Tomatoes (*Thakali*), pureed
1 stick	–	Cinnamon (*Pattai*)
3	–	Cloves (*Krambu*)
1 tsp.	–	Cumin (*Seeragam*)
1 tbsp.	–	Ginger garlic paste (*Inji poondu viluthu*)
3	–	Green chilies (*Pachai milagai*)
½ tsp.	–	Turmeric powder (*Manjal podi*)
2 tsp.	–	Coriander powder (*Malli podi*)
1 tsp.	–	Red chili powder (*Milagai podi*)
½ tsp.	–	Garam masala (*Garam masala podi*)
1 tsp.	–	Pepper powder (*Milagu thul*)
2 sprigs	–	Curry leaves (*Karuvapaellai*), finely chopped
1 cup	–	Coriander leaves (*Kothamali elai*), finely chopped
½ cup	–	Coconut milk (*Thengai paal*)
To taste	–	Salt (*Uppu*)
3 tbsp. + 3 tbsp.	–	Gingelly Oil (*Nalla ennai*)

Method:
1. In a large wok, heat 3 tbsp. oil
2. Add cloves and cinnamon
3. Add Cumin
4. Add 1-½ onions and saute till transparent
5. Cut the top and bottom ends of green chilies and add.
6. Add ginger garlic paste
7. Add turmeric powder, coriander powder and red chili powder
8. Add garam masala and salt
9. Add tomato puree
10. Cover and cook for 5 minutes
11. Add 2 cups of hot water and let it boil
12. Add coconut milk and let it cook for 5 minutes
13. Remove from heat and keep aside. The curry is ready
14. Beat the eggs with ½ onion finely chopped, curry leaves finely chopped, pepper powder and salt
15. In a large pan, heat 1 tbsp. oil
16. Pour out 1/3 rd of the egg mixture to make an omelette
17. Turn over and cook on both sides
18. Follow the same procedure to get 3 omelettes
19. Cut the omelettes into 2 pieces and add to the curry
20. Garnish with finely chopped coriander leaves

Tips: There are many ways of preparing the eggs
- Omelette cut into 2 pieces
- Boiled eggs cut into 2 halves
- Round omelette made in the kuzhi paniyaram maker
- Break the eggs directly into the curry and let them cook in the heat of the boiling curry

Everyday Poriyals

Strength and honour are her clothing; and she shall rejoice in time to come...

(Proverbs 31:25)

A typical South Indian lunch or dinner three-course meal consists of *Steamed Rice* (Main dish), *Kozhambu* (Curry) and a *Poriyal* (Side dish). 'Poriyal' is the dry vegetable component of the meal and is made with a single vegetable or a combination of complementing vegetables, which are either steam cooked, sautéed or deep-fried in oil. I used to be a compulsive non-vegetarian eater until my marriage. It was my husband's mother who introduced me to the wonderful world of vegetarian cooking with her numerous well-cooked and tasty vegetarian poriyal dishes. So this section is dedicated to her in gratitude.

Making a poriyal is very generalised and quite easy. The first step is to decide the cut of the vegetable, whether it is to be chopped finely, cut into cubes or strips. The next step is to temper a little oil with spices after which onions are sautéed in it. The vegetable is tossed in and allowed to steam cook covered under a lid. The last step is to add a little flavouring and dressing with grated coconut, curry leaves and coriander leaves. Usually, if curry leaves are added as a whole, the temptation is to discard them in the side of the plate uneaten. Hence, I always advocate chopping curry leaves and coriander leaves finely before adding, thus ensuring their complete consumption during a meal. My secret to tasty poriyals is to add a lot of onions (either chopped or julienned), which I have found to be an excellent taste enhancer. I also use only gingelly oil for all my cooking and a lite version of refined sunflower oil for all fried poriyals.

All the poriyals in this section can be also served with *Roti* and *Dhal*. *Potato fry* wins easily, hands down as the easiest and tastiest side dish that can not only be made in a jiffy but it also tastes great with rice and dhal or fried rice. A sure hit with guests. *Cauliflower fry* can be served with tomato ketchup as a starter in a party or get-together. *Avial* is my end-of-the-week poriyal as it is made with one vegetable of every type that is leftover or has survived that week in the refrigerator. I have presented just a few basic poriyal recipes in this section which I hope will form a base for you. Try some combinations on your own and do remember to note them down with your own notes and tips.

61. Carrot and Corn Poriyal

Ingredients:

2	–	Carrots (*Thuruviya carrot*), grated
½ cup	–	Corn (*Sollam*), boiled
1	–	Onions (*Vengayam*), finely chopped
3	–	Green chilies (*Pachai milagai*), finely chopped
3	–	Garlic (*Poondu*)
1 tsp.	–	Mustard (*Kadugu*)
1 tsp.	–	Black gram (*Ullutham parupu*)
1 tsp.	–	Cumin seeds (*Seeragam*)
3 tbsp.	–	Grated coconut (*Thuruviya thengai*)
2 sprigs	–	Curry leaves (*Karuvapaellai*), finely chopped
½ cup	–	Coriander leaves (*Kothamali elai*), finely chopped
2 tbsp.	–	Gingelly oil (*Nalla ennai*)
To taste	–	Salt (*Uppu*)

Method:
1. Grate the carrot finely
2. In a wok, heat oil
3. Season with mustard
4. When the mustard starts spluttering, add black gram and cumin seeds

5. Add onions and green chilies finely chopped
6. Add curry leaves finely chopped
7. Toss in the grated carrot and corn. Mix well
8. Simmer and sprinkle ¼ cup of water and close the wok with a lid
9. Cook for 5 minutes and add salt. Mix well
10. Cover and cook again for 10 minutes
11. Add coriander leaves finely chopped
12. Add grated coconut and mix well

Tip: While deep-frying, to reduce the amount of oil absorbed by the food when fried, add a pinch of salt to the oil before frying

62. Cabbage and Peas Poriyal

Ingredients:

½	–	Cabbage (*Muttai ghoz*), finely chopped
1 cup	–	Peas (*Pattani*)
1	–	Onions (*Vengayam*), finely chopped
3	–	Green chilies (*Pachai milagai*), finely chopped
1 tsp.	–	Mustard (*Kadugu*)
1 tsp.	–	Bengal gram (*Kadalai parupu*)
1 tsp.	–	Cumin seeds (*Seeragam*)
½ tsp.	–	Turmeric Powder (*Manjal podi*)
2 sprigs	–	Curry leaves (*Karuvapaellai*), finely chopped

1 cup	–	Coriander leaves (*Kothamali elai*), finely chopped
½ cup	–	Grated coconut (*Thuruviya thengai*)
2 tbsp.	–	Gingelly oil (*Nalla ennai*)
To taste	–	Salt (*Uppu*)

Method:
1. Soak peas in water to soften them for ½ hour
2. In a wok, heat oil
3. Season with mustard
4. When the mustard starts spluttering, add bengal gram and cumin
5. Add onions and green chilies finely chopped
6. Add curry leaves finely chopped
7. Toss in the cabbage, finely chopped
8. Add peas and mix well
9. Simmer and sprinkle ¼ cup of water. Cover the wok with a lid and let the cabbage and peas cook
10. After 5 minutes add turmeric powder
11. Add salt. Mix well
12. Cover and cook again for 10 minutes
13. Add coriander leaves
14. Add grated coconut and mix well

Tip: The same recipe can be used to make other dishes by substituting peas with either grated carrot or roasted green gram

63. Cauliflower Fry

Ingredients:

1	–	Cauliflower (*Poo ghoz*), cut into small florets
½ cup	–	Bengal gram flour (*Kadala mavu*)
¼ cup	–	Corn flour (*Solla mavu*)
¼ tsp.	–	Baking soda (*Aapa soda*)
½ tsp.	–	Turmeric powder (*Manjal podi*)
½ tsp.	–	Red chili powder (*Milagai podi*)
To taste	–	Salt (*Uppu*)
3 cups	–	Refined sunflower oil for frying (*Poripathuku ennai*)

Method:
1. In a large pot, boil 2 cups of water and salt
2. Add the cauliflower florets and cook for one bubble
3. Drain the water and keep the cauliflower florets aside
4. Heat oil for frying
5. Make a thick batter of bengal gram flour, corn flour, soda, turmeric powder, red chili powder, salt and water
6. Dip the florets in the batter and deep fry in hot oil until golden brown
7. Serve hot with tomato ketchup

Tip: Soak the cauliflower florets in salted hot water for 10 minutes to remove tiny worms, if any

64. Potato Fry

Ingredients:

2	–	Potatoes (*Urulaikkilangu*), cut into small cubes
1 tsp.	–	Mustard (*Kadugu*)
1 tsp.	–	Cumin seeds (*Seeragam*)
½ tsp.	–	Turmeric powder (*Manjal podi*)
2 tsp.	–	Coriander powder (*Malli podi*)
1 tsp.	–	Red chili powder (*Milagai podi*)
¼ tsp.	–	Garam Masala (*Garam masala podi*)
2 tbsp.	–	Gingelly oil (*Nalla ennai*)
To taste	–	Salt (*Uppu*)

Method:

1. De-skin the potatoes and cut into small cubes
2. Heat oil in a wok
3. Season with mustard
4. When the mustard starts spluttering, add cumin seeds
5. Toss in the potato cubes and mix well so that they are coated in oil
6. Add turmeric powder, coriander powder, red chili powder
7. Add garam masala
8. Simmer and cover the wok with a lid and cook for 15 minutes. Stir once in every 5 minutes to ensure uniform cooking of the potatoes

Tip: Store potatoes, onions and garlic in open space with good air circulation to prevent it from rotting. But do not store onions and potatoes together in the same basket or container

65. Beetroot Poriyal

Ingredients:

1	–	Beetroot (*Akkaara kizhangu*), chopped into tiny cubes
1 cup	–	White chickpeas (*Vellai konda kadalai*)
1	–	Onions (*Vengayam*), finely chopped
3	–	Green chilies (*Pachai milagai*), finely chopped
3	–	Garlic (*Poondu*)
1 tsp.	–	Mustard (*Kadugu*)
1 tsp.	–	Black gram (*Ullutham parupu*)
1 tsp.	–	Cumin seeds (*Seeragam*)
3 tbsp.	–	Grated coconut (*Thuruviya thengai*)
2 sprigs	–	Curry leaves (*Karuvapaellai*), finely chopped
½ cup	–	Coriander leaves (*Kothamali elai*), finely chopped
To taste	–	Salt (*Uppu*)
2 tbsp.	–	Gingelly oil (*Nalla ennai*)

Method:

1. Soak the white chickpeas for 8 hours. Pressure cook for 8 whistles or till they soften. Keep aside to cool
2. Wash the beetroot well to remove any dirt. Remove the skin by cutting with a knife

3. Grate the beetroot or else cut into tiny cubes. This will enable the beetroot to cook fast
4. In a kadai, heat oil
5. Season with mustard
6. When the mustard starts spluttering, add black gram and cumin
7. Add onion and curry leaves. Saute for one minute
8. When the onions turn transparent, add garlic pods
9. Add the beetroot and mix well
10. Simmer and sprinkle ¼ cup of water and close the wok with a lid
11. After 5 minutes, add salt to taste
12. Add the cooked white chickpeas and mix well
13. Cover again and let it cook well
14. Add grated coconut and coriander leaves. Remove from the fire

Tip: The same recipe can be used for preparing a variety of other vegetables such as Beans poriyal, Cauliflower poriyal, Carrot poriyal or Cabbage poriyal by substituting beetroot with the vegetable. The rest of the ingredients and method remains the same

66. Kovakai Poriyal

Ingredients:

2 cups	–	Ivy gourd (*Kovakai*), sliced
1 tsp.	–	Mustard (*Kadugu*)

½ tsp.	–	Black gram (*Ullutham parupu*)
½ tsp.	–	Cumin seeds (*Seeragam*)
1	–	Onions (*Vengayam*), finely chopped
2	–	Garlic (*Poondu*)
½ tsp.	–	Turmeric powder (*Manjal podi*)
1 tbsp.	–	Red chili powder (*Milagai podi*)
2 sprigs	–	Curry leaves (*Karuvapaellai*)
To taste	–	Salt (*Uppu*)
2 tbsp.	–	Gingelly oil (*Nalla ennai*)

Method:
1. Wash the kovakai well. Cut longitudinally into 4 or slice into rounds
2. Heat oil in a wok
3. Season with mustard and black gram
4. Add cumin seeds
5. Add onions
6. Add curry leaves
7. Add garlic
8. Toss in the kovakai pieces
9. Add turmeric powder, red chili powder and salt
10. Sprinkle water and cook under a lid for 15 minutes

Tip: To freshen stale vegetables, soak them for one hour in a bowl of cold water to which lime juice has been added

67. Akuri

Ingredients:

3	–	Eggs (*Muttai*)
1	–	Onions (*Vengayam*), finely chopped
1	–	Tomatoes (*Thakali*), finely chopped
½	–	Capsicum (*Kudai milagai*), finely chopped
1 sprig	–	Curry leaves (*Karuvapaellai*), finely chopped
½ cup	–	Coriander leaves (*Kothamali elai*), finely chopped
¼ tsp.	–	Turmeric powder (*Manjal podi*)
½ tsp.	–	Red chili powder (*Milagai podi*)
½ tsp.	–	Pepper powder (*Milagu thul*)
½ tsp.	–	Ginger garlic paste (*Inji poondu viluthu*)
1 tbsp.	–	Cream (*Paal eidu*)
2 tbsp.	–	Butter (*Vennai*)
To taste	–	Salt (*Uppu*)

Method:

1. Beat the eggs well with the cream until light and fluffy
2. In a large wok, melt the butter
3. Add onions, capsicum and curry leaves, all finely chopped
4. When the onions are sauted to transparency, add the ginger garlic paste
5. Add tomatoes and mix well
6. Simmer and add turmeric powder, red chili powder, pepper powder and salt
7. On simmer, add the egg batter and scramble the eggs finely
8. Add coriander leaves
9. Serve hot with bread toast or as a side dish to rice and dhal

Tip: To test if eggs are good or bad, drop them into a bowl of water. Eggs that are good will sink to the bottom whereas eggs that have gone bad will float in the water

68. Avial

Ingredients:

2	–	Brinjals (*Katharikai*), cut long
2	–	Cucumber (*Vellarikai*), cut long
2	–	Raw bananas (*Valaka*), cut long
2	–	Potatoes (*Urulaikkilangu*), cut long
2	–	Carrots (*Manjai mulangi*), cut long
½	–	Beans (*Vithayavarai*), cut long
½ cup	–	Pumpkin (*Pusanikai*), cut long
2	–	Drumsticks (*Murungakai*), cut long
½	–	Coconut, grated (*Thuruviya thengai*)
2 cups	–	Sour curds (*Pulicha thayir*)
½ tsp.	–	Turmeric powder (*Manjal podi*)
1 tsp.	–	Cumin seeds (*Seeragam*)
5	–	Green chilies (*Pachai milagai*)
1 tsp.	–	Mustard (*Kadugu*)
1 tsp.	–	Black gram (*Ullutham parupu*)
2 sprigs	–	Curry leaves (*Karuvapaellai*), finely chopped
3 tbsp.	–	Coconut oil (*Thengai ennai*)

Method:

1. Cut all vegetables into 2" strips. Remove skin if necessary
2. Place all the vegetables except cucumber and brinjal in the pressure cooker and steam cook for 2 whistles. Remove the vegetables and drain the water, if any. Keep aside.

3. In a wok heat coconut oil. Season with mustard and black gram
4. Add curry leaves
5. Add brinjal and cucumber and stir-fry for a few minutes.
6. Sprinkle water and cover the wok with a lid. Let the vegetables cook for 5 minutes on simmer
7. Add the pressure cooked vegetables, salt and turmeric powder
8. Grind coconut, green chilies and cumin seeds together. Add a little hot water and grind again
9. Add the ground paste to the vegetables. Simmer on low heat for a few minutes
10. Switch off the stove and cool slightly
11. Add curds when cooled
12. Mix well

Tip: Instead of vegetables, a non-vegetarial avail can be made into *Fish Avial* following the same recipe. For this, use small and slender fish varieites like Sardines (*Challa meen*) or Anchovy (*Nethily*).

69. Cucumber Poriyal

Ingredients:

2	–	Cucumber (*Vellarikai*)
2	–	Green chilies (*Pachai milagai*), finely chopped
1 tsp.	–	Mustard (*Kadugu*)
1 tsp.	–	Black gram (*Ullutham parupu*)

½ tsp.	–	Turmeric powder (*Manjal podi*)
1 sprig	–	Curry leaves (*Karuvapaellai*)
½ cup	–	Grated coconut (*Thuruviya thengai*)
1 cup	–	Fresh Curds (*Thayir*)
1 tbsp.	–	Gingelly oil (*Nalla ennai*)

Method:
1. Wash the cucumber well. Peel the skin and cut longitudinally into 4 long strips. Remove the seeds and cut into cubes
2. Heat oil in a wok
3. Season with mustard and black gram
4. Add green chilies and curry leaves
5. Toss in the cucumber cubes
6. Add turmeric powder and salt
7. Sprinkle water and cook under a lid for 15 minutes till the cucumber softens
8. Add grated coconut and remove from the fire. Allow to cool well
9. When it has cooled fully, add curds and mix well

Tip: To make good and thick curds, take a glass bowl and set 1 tsp. of culture into warm milk, at room temperature. Cover and let it rest in a warm place for 5–8 hours

70. Beans Poriyal

Ingredients:

2 cups	–	Beans (*Vithayavarai*), finely chopped
1	–	Onions (*Vengayam*), finely chopped
1	–	Tomatoes (*Thakali*), finely chopped
6	–	Garlic (*Poondu*)
1 tsp.	–	Mustard (*Kadugu*)
1 tsp.	–	Cumin seeds (*Seeragam*)
½ tsp.	–	Turmeric powder (*Manjal podi*)
2 tsp.	–	Coriander powder (*Malli podi*)
1 tsp.	–	Red chili powder (*Milagai podi*)
2 sprigs	–	Curry leaves (*Karuvapaellai*), finely chopped
To taste	–	Salt (*Uppu*)
2 tbsp.	–	Gingelly oil (*Nalla ennai*)

Method:

1. Heat oil in a wok
2. Season with mustard and cumin
3. Saute onions till transparent
4. Add curry leaves finely chopped
5. Add garlic
6. Add tomatoes
7. Add beans
8. Add turmeric powder, coriander powder, red chili powder and salt
9. Cover and cook under a lid for 20 minutes till the beans has cooked well. Every 5 minutes open and mix well
10. Serve hot with rice or chapatti and dhal

Note: The same recipe can be used to make other poriyas with Ladies finger (*Vendaka*), Bitter gourd (*Pavakai*) or Flat beans (*Avarakai*) instead of beans

Tip: While frying fish, chicken or mutton, add a few sprigs of curry leaves to the hot oil for better flavour and aroma

Hobby Time – Baking

Who can find a virtuous woman?... For her price is far above rubies

(Proverbs 31:10)

There is nothing more comforting and welcoming than the aroma of freshly baked bread or a cake. That's home to me. When I think of baking I am reminded of Enid Blyton's books that I read as a child and still continue to read for inspiration. She is rightly known as the *Goddess of Fictional Food* for she could make even bread and butter sound delicious like an exotic dish. As a young reader, all my five senses were stimulated towards hunger for baked goods. I mean, take for example, *The Famous Five*, which were the ultimate food-nostalgia series of books. They set a standard in picnics that has never been equaled! What with their small but lip-smacking ginger buns, melt-in-the-mouth shortbread biscuits, mouth-watering large chocolate sponges, yummy hot new-made scone!

Baking is one of the best hobbies ever. There is definitely something fancy and fashionable while referring to baking as a hobby. The four basic ingredients of baking are Flour, Butter, Sugar and Baking powder and with these in hand it could be a lifetime adventure in discovering and trying out new recipes for breads, cakes, cookies, pastries pies, tarts, quiches, cookies, scones, pretzels, crackers etc.,

My sister specializes in baking the most amazing cakes I have ever tasted in my life. So this section is dedicated to her. There's a cake for each day of the year, ranging from cupcakes to the seven colour rainbow cake or battenburg cake, the classic Genoese sponge, black forest cake, novelty swiss roll, angel cake, layer cakes, upside down cakes, the devil's food cake (a cake so delicious that it is termed so) and of course everyone's favourite – the all occasion chocolate cake. Yummy! In the biscuit world, a true biscuit will make a decided snapping noise when broken into half whereas a cookie is softer and thicker than a biscuit. There are different types of Pastries like:

1. **Puff pastry:** Apple cinnamon roses, Palmiers, Turnovers, Puffs, Bouchees etc.,
2. **Danish pastry:** Twists, Cinnamon roll, Butterfly rolls, cresents, crowns, slips etc.,

3. **Short crust pastry:** Welsh cheese cakes, Cottage pies, Tartlets
4. **Flaky pastry:** Pathir Pheni or Chiroti

Go on! Get an oven and start baking. Get together with cousins or friends and host a bake sale this weekend. Enjoy!

Baking Utensils – Cake Tins

A simple sponge cake can be made to look exotic by using a different shape cake tin. Also depending on the occasion, choose a cake tin to fit the theme. For eg. Use a tree shaped tin for Christmas or a heart shaped tin for Valentine's day and so on. Below are a few collectibles that I recommend.

Measuring Tools

The first lesson in baking is to measure the amount of ingredients specified accurately and correctly. Always follow the recipe to a T. For eg. In the case of teaspoon and tablespoon measures, check if the measures are 'heaped', 'rounded' or 'leveled'. If it is not specified, read spoon and cup measurements as 'level'.

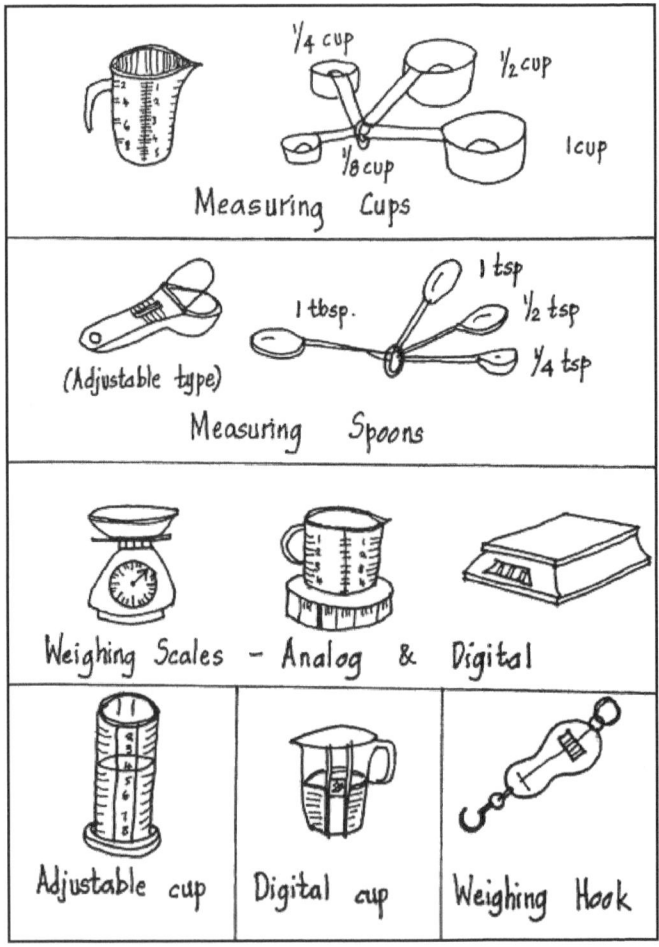

Types of Bread

Most of us associate breadmaking as something that only a baker makes in a bakery. But, believe me, bread making at home is relatively simple and once you have baked and eaten your own bread, you will never be satisfied with a shop-bought loaf. There are many varieties of bread; a few are shown below. The constant companion for bread is butter and jam but don't hesitate to experiment and invent your own sandwich.

There are many ways to eat bread. You can eat it as it is or make it into a sandwich. Bread can be toasted or fried. Bread forms the base ingredient for Bread pudding, Bread Gulab Jamun, Bread bajji, Croquettes etc.,. Bread can also be eaten and it tastes really good with Vegetable Kurma, Chicken curry or Chicken in white sauce.

Types of Cakes

Is there a cake for every occasion? I do believe there is!

A cake is celebration food and they make the occasion more memorable. Birthdays, Weddings, anniversaries, event markings etc, all centre around the cake. For eg. the Yule log and Spice cake mark Christmas,... a multi-tiered cake means a wedding,...a chocolate cake means a birthday and so on.

The basic ingredients of cakes are flour, butter and sugar. Depending on the type of cake, we also add eggs, baking powder and vanilla essence. Seasonal frutis and food colouring can also be incorportated into the recipe for variations. Cakes can be eaten as they are but the icing makes it not only more delicious but beautiful as well.

Types of Cookies and Biscuits

Though both cookies and biscuits are both baked products and use the same base ingredients like flour, sugar and butter, a cookie is slightly different from a biscuit. A cookie is sweet, softer and can include chocolate chips, nuts or raisins in the recipe to enhance the flavour. On the other hand, a biscuit is crisp and can be sweet or savoury.

The dry ingredients for cakes, cookies and biscuits are the same but differ in measures for wet ingredients. For cakes, the liquid batter must fold when poured out into a tin. For cookies and biscuits, the dough must be kneadable and rollable. The dough can be folded for different shapes or you can use cookie cutters.

Types of Pastries

The basic ingredients used for making pastry are flour, ice-cold butter, a pinch of salt and ice cold water. To make a pastry, the technique is rolling out the dough and folding multiple times till layers are formed. Pastries are a delight for a baking enthusiast because of the countless variations possible with different shapes and fillings, both sweet and savoury.

71. Brownies

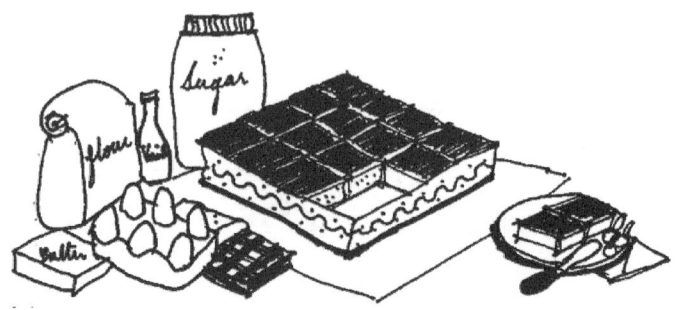

Who can resist a chocolate fudge brownie? In fact, the batter itself is to die for. If you can get past licking the bowl and spoon clean before baking, then the result is a perfect crisp, crackly top and a super fudgy, gooey and chewy centred brownie. Yum!!

Pure...... Chocolate...... Heaven!

Ingredients:

¾ cup	–	Flour (*Maida mavu*)
100 g	–	Butter (*Vennai*)
1 cup	–	Powdered sugar (*Poditha sarkarai*)
2	–	Eggs (*Muttai*)
6 tbsp.	–	Cocoa powder (*Cocoa thul*)
1	–	Chocolate bar (*Sakalete*), melted for topping the brownies
½ cup	–	Walnuts (*Akrut*), chopped

Method:

1. Whisk together eggs and sugar in a bowl with a beater
2. Melt butter in a saucepan on simmer. Do not over heat
3. Add cocoa and mix well
4. Add this mixture to the whisked eggs
5. Fold in the flour gently
6. Pour into a well greased and floured square cake tin
7. Bake in a pre-heated oven at 180' for 25 mins

8. Melt a chocolate bar using a double boiler
9. Spread the melted chocolate on the brownies
10. Sprinkle walnuts over the brownies and cool. Cut into squares when cold

Tip: Always prepare the cake tin before mixing the baking ingredients. Once the baking mix is prepared it must be transferred into the tin and baked in the oven immediately for a good effect. Do not keep the mix out for a long time.

72. Banana Carrot Cake

What happens when vegetable meets fruit? The result is a light and fresh cake, perfect for evening tea with friends.

Ingredients:

2	–	Ripe green bananas, mashed (*Vazhai pazham*)
¼ cup	–	Grated carrot (*Thuruviya carrot*)
1-½ cups	–	Flour (*Maida mavu*)
100 g	–	Butter (*Vennai*)
1 cup	–	Powdered Sugar (*Poditha sarkarai*)
1	–	Egg (*Muttai*)
1 tsp.	–	Baking powder
1 tbsp.	–	Grated rind of lime (*Thuruviya elumicha thol*)
2 tbsp.	–	Boiled milk (*Kothikavaitha Paal*) Use more, if required

Method:
1. Beat butter and powdered sugar
2. Add egg
3. Add lemon rind
4. Add mashed bananas and beat till smooth
5. Sift flour with baking powder
6. Fold in the sifted flour and grated carrot into the batter
7. Add milk to get folding consistency
8. Pour into a well greased and floured cake tin
9. Bake in a pre-heated oven at 180˚ for 45 minutes
10. Serve with a generous dripping of hot chocolate sauce

Tip: Never store cakes and biscuits together in the same tin. The biscuits will take up the moisture from the cake and lose their crispness. Cakes must be wrapped in aluminum foil before storing in an airtight container. This keeps them soft and moist. Biscuits must be stored in dry, airtight tins.

73. Pineapple upside Down Cake

This recipe can be used during a women's fellowship in your home or you could have a group baking activity in your club. The Pineapple upside down cake is always a winner and never fails to impress!

Ingredients:
1-½ cups	–	Flour (*Maida mavu*)
100 g	–	Butter (*Vennai*), melted

1-½ cups	–	Powdered sugar (*Poditha sarkarai*)
2	–	Eggs (*Muttai*)
1 tsp.	–	Baking powder
½ tsp.	–	Cinnamon powder (*Ilavankappattai thul*)
6 tbsp.	–	Warm boiled milk (*Kothikavaitha Paal*)

Topping.

6 slices	–	Pineapple (*Annasi pazham*)
6	–	Glace cherries (*Sela pazham*)
½ cup	–	Powdered sugar (*Poditha sarkarai*)

Method:

1. Core the pineapple slices and dip both sides in ½ cup powdered sugar. Keep aside for 20 minutes
2. Grease and flour a cake tin. Arrange the pineapple slices on the base and fill the centres with cherries

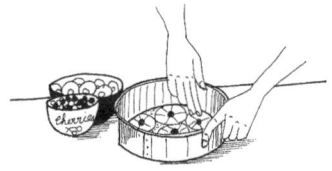

3. Cream butter and sugar till light and creamy
4. Whisk the eggs well and add gradually, beating all the time
5. Sift flour, cinnamon powder and baking powder together 3 times
6. Fold in the flour mixture alternating with milk
7. Pour the batter over the pineapple base taking care not to disturb the pineapple arrangement

8. Bake at 205°C for 40 minutes

9. When the cake has cooled, invert it onto a cake base or plate.

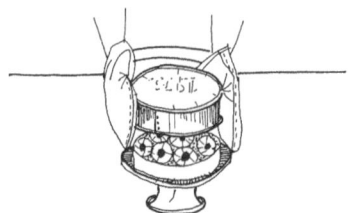

10. Voila! The pineapple slices are now at the top!!!

Tip: To check if the cake is done, pierce a knife through the cake. If it comes out clean, it is done. But, never unnecessarily open the oven door fully while a cake is baking. An inrush of cold air into the oven will cause the cake to rise unevenly and even sink

74. Apple Sponge

I have made this recipe so many times as it has the simplest list of ingredients and is so easy to make yet so delicious. The sponge is snow white and when overturned has the most beautiful caramelised apple slices on display. An absolute delight and a delicious delight at teatime especially if served hot, straight from the oven

Ingredients:

1	–	Apple (*Arathi pazham*)
1 cup	–	Flour (*Maida mavu*)
50 g	–	Butter (*Vennai*), melted

½ cup	–	Powdered sugar (*Poditha sarkarai*)
1	–	Egg (*Muttai*)
1 tsp.	–	Baking powder
5 tbsp.	–	Hot boiled milk (*Kothikavaitha Paal*)

Method:

1. Skin the apple and cut very thin slices. Arrange the slices in an 8" well greased and floured baking tray
2. Sprinkle powdered sugar on top evenly. Keep aside
3. Beat butter and powdered sugar well
4. Add the egg and beat again
5. Sift flour with baking powder. Fold this mixture into the egg mixture lightly.
6. Add hot milk to get a folding consistency when poured out
7. Pour the batter over the apples taking care not to disturb the arrangement. Tap the sides of the tin gently to even out the batter

8. Bake in a pre-heated oven at 180' for 45 minutes
9. Allow to cool and turn over onto a serving plate so that the apple slices come on top

Tip: While butter, eggs and sugar must be whisked and beaten well, flour must be only folded in lightly to get a light and fluffy cake.

79. Date Cake

This is a simple but mouth-watering cake to make taking advantage of the goodness of dates. Well, what is simple about this cake is that you simply cannot say no to this one! Tastes best with a sprinking of icing sugar on top and served with a glass of warm milk at breakfast. It can also be packed as a mid-day snack treat for your kids in their tiffin box.

Ingredients:

2 cups	–	Dates (*Perichampazham*), very finely chopped
2 cups	–	Flour (*Maida mavu*)
100 g	–	Butter (*Vennai*)
1-½ cups	–	Powdered sugar (*Poditha sarkarai*)
3	–	Eggs (*Muttai*)
1 tsp.	–	Baking soda (*Aapa soda*)
1 tsp.	–	Baking powder
1 tsp.	–	Vanilla essence (*Vanilla saarai*)
1 cup	–	Boiling water
½ cup	–	Cashewnuts (*Mundiri*)

Method:

1. Soak the chopped dates in boiling water with baking soda for 3 hours. Drain the water and keep aside.
2. Cream butter and sugar well
3. Add well-beaten eggs and vanilla essence. Whisk well

4. Add the dates and gently mix. Do not beat or whisk
5. Sift flour and baking powder three times. Gently fold in this dry mix into the wet ingredients
6. Add cashew nuts finely chopped and dusted in flour
7. Pour out the batter into a large well greased and floured baking tray. Tap gently to even out the batter smoothly
8. Bake in a pre-heated oven at 180' for 45 minutes

Tip: Dried fruits and nuts must be dusted in flour and added last to the cake batter or else they will sink to the bottom of the cake instead of being spread out evenly throughout the cake

76. Chocolate Cake

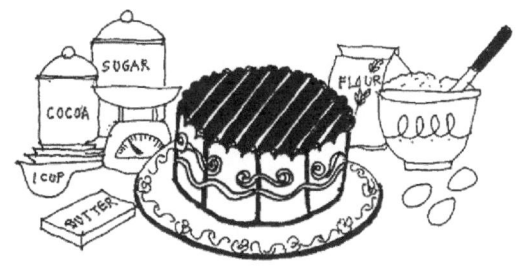

A "traditional" chocolate cake with chocolate ganache dripping on the sides and the glow of candles making it even lovelier, makes it the perfect cake for a birthday or an anniversary. This cake can be made with cocoa powder or cooking chocolate. Delicious frostings and icings like butter cream, coffee icing etc., can be spreak on top or inbetween layers to enhance the taste of the cake. By adding extra ingredients and multiple layers to the cake, other variants of the chocolate cake can be made such as Black forest cake, Devils food cake, Ding Dong, Fudge cake and so on.

Ingredients:

1 cup	–	Flour (*Maida mavu*)
100 g	–	Butter (*Vennai*)
1 cup	–	Powdered sugar (*Poditha sarkarai*)
3	–	Eggs (*Muttai*)

1 tsp.	–	Baking powder
½ tsp	–	Vanilla essence (*Vanilla saarai*)
5 tbsp	–	Cocoa powder (*Cocoa thul*)

Method:
1. Separate eggs
2. Beat the egg whites till light and fluffy. Keep aside
3. Beat melted butter and powdered sugar well
4. Add egg yolks and beat well
5. Add vanilla essence and beat well
6. Add egg whites and mix well
7. Sift together flour, baking powder and cocoa three times
8. Fold in the flour mixture gently
9. Pour into a well greased and floured cake tin
10. Bake in a pre-heated oven at 180' for 25 minutes
11. Serve with the icing of your choice like butter cream or chocolate icing

Tip: Never add eggs to hot melted butter. The eggs will scramble and the butter will curdle. This will form light streaks on top of the cake. You can remedy this by adding 1 tsp. of flour to the butter before adding the eggs or waiting for the butter to cool slightly.

77. Dark Chocolate Biscuit Cheesecake

Cheesecake is one of the tastiest cakes and tops the list of 'most wanted cakes' despite its' high calorie content. It is usually made with a refrigerated cold biscuit crumble base topped with a rich cream cheese cake layer finished off nicely with a contrast blueberry jam layer. The biscuit layer in this recipe has been substituted with a dark chocolate biscuit layer to vary the taste. But believe me, it is mouth watering and you cannot resist taking a second, third or even a fourth helping!

Ingredients:

2 cups	–	Cream cheese or hung curd, made from
2	–	litres of boiled milk made into curds
12	–	Dark chocolate biscuits
1 tbsp.	–	Butter (*Vennai*)
½ cup	–	Powdered sugar (*Poditha sarkarai*)
2	–	Eggs (*Muttai*)
½ tsp.	–	Vanilla essence (*Vanilla saarai*)
½ cup	–	Fresh cream (*Paal eidu*)
¼ cup	–	Boiled milk (*Kothikavaitha Paal*)

Method:

1. Lightly crumble the dark chocolate biscuits in the food processor with 1 tbsp. butter
2. Keep aside ½ cup of biscuit crumble and spread the rest into the base of a well-greased pie tin and press down well. Refrigerate for 1 hour
3. To make cream cheese, make 2 litres of milk into curds. Tie the curds in a muslin cloth and hang over a dish for about 4 hours. The whey water will drip into the dish gradually leaving the residual thick cream cheese or 'hung curd' in the cloth

4. Beat the cream cheese well in the blender
5. Add vanilla essence and blend
6. Add powdered sugar, milk and cream and blend well
7. Whisk eggs and add

8. Pour this batter onto the pie dish gently over the biscuit base

9. Sprinkle ½ cup of biscuit crumble on top
10. Bake in a preheated oven at 160' for 40 minutes
11. This cheese cake tastes good when refrigerated and cold

Tip: To make a good cheesecake, cream cheese should be fresh and not sour. The cream cheese should be at room temperature to get a soft and fluffy texture

78. Coffee Cup Cakes

A cupcake is a mini cake served in a paper cup! They use the same recipe as regular large cakes but are baked in individual muffin tins or patty cases and they take just a few minutes to bake, Cupcakes are perfect for parties where you want to serve cake but there is no cake-cutting event or when you are expecting a large number of invitees. They are ideal for potluck tea parties, community events and office parties etc. For a bridal or baby shower you can make theme cup cakes with different icings, toppings and fondant. You can serve them on a tray or jazz up the celebration by stacking them in a multi-tiered cupcake stand.

Ingredients:

1-¼ cups	–	Flour (*Maida mavu*)
170 g	–	Butter (*Vennai*)
1 cup	–	Powdered sugar (*Poditha sarkarai*)
4	–	Eggs (*Muttai*)
2 tsp.	–	Baking powder
2 tsp.	–	Vanilla essence (*Vanilla saarai*)
2 tsp.	–	Instant coffee powder (*Kaapi thul*)
1-½ cups	–	Hot boiled milk (*Kothikavaitha Paal*)
¼ cup	–	Chocolate chips (*Sakalete thundugal*)

Method:
1. Beat butter and sugar till stiff
2. Whisk eggs till light and fluffy
3. Add to the butter mixture
4. Add vanilla essence
5. Sift flour, baking powder and coffee powder 3 times and add
6. Add ½ of the chocolate chips
7. Add milk to get dropping consistency
8. Put spoonfulls of batter to fill only ¾th of the paper cake cups. This is to give allowance for the cupcakes to rise and bake without spilling over
9. Sprinkle the remaining ½ of the chocolate chips on top
10. Place the paper cups in a preheated oven and bake at 180˚ for 20 minutes
11. When cool, decorate with butter cream icing and sprinkles

Tip: Always separate eggs one by one in a bowl before mixing them together. There is a chance one or two eggs may be spoilt. Also make sure the bowl in which the egg whites are beaten is immaculately clean without any trace of butter or egg yolks.

79. Chocolate Chip Cookies

Cookies are a gourmet traveller's companion on outdoor outings and travels. That's because cookies are non-messy and have a longer shelf life than other foodstuff. They are served with beverages such as milk, coffee or tea. In this recipe I have made a traditional cookie with chocolate chips. Irresistable! The same recipe can be used to make other variants by substituting the chocolate chips with cashewnuts, dates, walnuts, almonds and dried frutis.

Ingredients:

1–¼ cups	–	Flour (*Maida mavu*)
100 g	–	Butter (*Vennai*)
¾ cup	–	Brown sugar (*Palupu sarkarai*)
1	–	Eggs (*Muttai*)
1 tsp.	–	Baking powder
1 tsp.	–	Vanilla essence (*Vanilla saarai*)
2-½ tsp.	–	Cocoa powder (*Cocoa thul*)
1/3 cup	–	Chocolate chips (*Sakalete thundugal*), white and brown

Method:

1. In a bowl, sift flour, baking powder and cocoa together three times
2. In a mixer, blend butter and sugar well
3. Add egg and vanilla essence. Blend till smooth
4. Add this to the flour mixture and knead into a soft dough

5. Make around 15 small balls. Flatten out each ball in your palm to form a round cookie shape
6. Grease a baking tray with a little butter. Dust with maida. Place the cookies on them leaving 1" space between each cookie
7. Sprinkle chocolate chips over the cookies and press into them lightly
8. Bake in a pre-heated oven at 180' for 10 minutes

Tip: Always bake cookies and biscuits in the centre of the oven on the middle rack to give them even baking and colouring

80. Apple Cinnamon Roses

Is it a rose? Is it an apple? This pastry snack will keep your guests guessing even after they take a bite into it. Using simple and straight forward baking ingredients but fashioning them out cleverly so that apple slices resemble rose petals will earn you more praise adjectives for a simple baking effort. This dish is good sweet pass-around starter rather than a dessert.

Ingredients:

1	–	Apple (*Arathi pazham*)
50 g	–	Butter (*Vennai*), melted
¼ cup + 1 tbsp	–	Sugar (*Sarkarai*)
1	–	Egg (*Muttai*)
1" stick	-	Cinnamon (*Pattai*)
2 tsp.	–	Water for sealing the edges
6	–	Puff pastry sheets

Puff pastry:

1 cup	–	Flour (*Maida mavu*)
50 g + 50 g	–	Butter cubes (*Vennai*), ice cold
A pinch	–	Salt (*Uppu*)
2 tbsp.	–	Ice cold water

Method:

To make the puff pastry:

1. In a deep bowl, take sifted flour. Add salt
2. Rub 50 g of cold butter cubes into the flour to resemble breadcrumbs.
3. Sprinkle water and knead into a soft dough
4. On a floured board, roll out the dough into a rectangle shape of ½" thickness

5. Spread 25 g of butter cubes on the roll and fold up as shown in the drawing below:

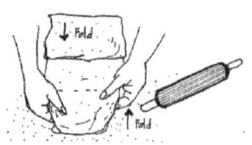

6. Wrap the roll in cling wrap or a plastic sheet and refrigerate for 20 minutes
7. After 20 minutes, roll out again a rectangular shape of ½" thickness.
8. Spread the remaining 25 g of butter cubes on the roll and fold up before
9. Return to the refrigerator for another 1 hour.

10. After 1 hour, cut the roll into 6 squares of 3" x 3" as shown below:

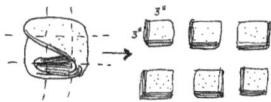

11. Roll out the 6 squares into thin and long rectangular strips of dimensions 3" x 8" as shown below. The puff pastry is ready for use

To make the roses:

12. Grind sugar and the cinnamon to a fine powder. Keep aside
13. Cut the apple into two. Remove the core. No need to remove the skin. Turn over and slice into very thin slices along its breadth
14. Place the sliced apples in a bowl of cold water. Add a tbsp. of sugar to it. Lightly heat or microwave for three minutes. Do not boil. This is to make the apples pliable and a soft to roll later on. Drain the water and pat dry the apple slices with a tea towel
15. Lay out the puff pastry strips. Spread melted butter on top using a brush. Sprinkle powdered sugar and cinnamon powder generously on top
16. Place the sliced apples along one long edge of the pastry, slightly overlapping each slice and projecting out a little over the edge as shown below:

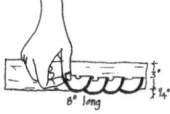

17. Fold the bottom half of the pastry so that it contains the apple slices

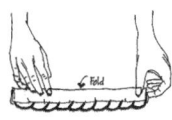

18. Beat together egg and water in a bowl
19. Brush along the pastry with this egg wash. Sprinkle more sugar and cinnamon powder on top

20. Starting from one end, roll the pastry lightly to form a rose shape as shown below. Seal the edge with water. Brush the outer surface with egg wash.

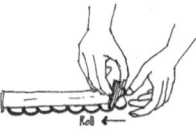

21. Place the roses in a buttered muffin tray

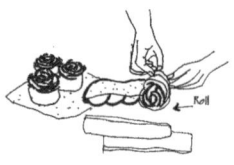

22. Bake in a preheated oven at 190' for 45 minutes to get aromatic and beautiful apple cinnamon roses!!!

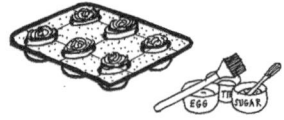

23. Sprinkle icing sugar on top just before serving

Tip: Dry ingredients like flour, cocoa, baking powder and cinnamon powder must be sifted together three times to get an even distribution of ingredients and also to add volume in the cake. But this dry mix must be just folded in lightly into the wet mix of ingredients.

Summer Holidays

*"She looketh well to the ways of her household,
and eateth not the bread of idleness"*
— Proverbs 31:27

When I think of summer, I think of holidays and a time to be free... a time for friends and family. I think of it as a gift I give myself after a long year of hard work, late nights and very early mornings. A lot of people go away for the summer to a far away beach resort or to the cool mountainside as a get away. For me, I love my home, my family and my kitchen. There's nowhere else I'd rather be during a summer holiday than at home...nothing beats that. To be in the comfort of my own home, tucked in my cozy bed in comfortable clothes, a good book in one hand, juice in the other, and golden oldies music playing in the background... That is my idea of a summer holiday. I dedicate this section to my brother who was my childhood playmate and made holidays at home so much fun.

So while at home, I make best use of the hot summer sun and the holidays for canning and preservation ideas. Suddenly the sun with the hottest heat is my new best friend for making pickles and masalas, sterilizing bottles before pickles, jams and juices are preserved in them and also for bleaching yellowed cookware. The heat is not always good, as you can get terribly dehydrated during the summer and fall ill. So drinking a lot of juices especially *Limejuice* is good and for this, I have given you a simple recipe. *Raw mango juice* is especially very good for the summer and prevents dehydration. I make the most of the mango season during summer and have presented a few recipes for *Mango kulfi, Mango juices* and *Mango cake* in this section... I would also advise you to get your very own ice cream maker. This way you can enjoy making and eating ice creams and kulfis from your own kitchen.

I enjoy making and bottling pickles. I think of pickling like a friendship preserved for many years. To last a long time, at the budding of a friendship, care must be taken to do the right things. The same applies to pickle making. Utmost care must be taken to avoid any moisture and also the right proportion of preservatives must be added. A careless word in a friendship is moisture in a pickle and that can spoil it forever. I have a number of good old friends; Kiten, Esther, Preeti, Priti, Prabhu and like a good old friend, the best pickles are the oldest ones.

Types of Preserves

Preserves are foodstuff preserved in salt or sugar. They are very easy to make. Mashing and cooking fruits with sugar make jams. Diluting fruit syrups and then combining with sugar syrup make juices and squashes. Ketchups are made by slow cooking tomato puree in spices.

Types of Beverages

There's a beverage for every weather! There's a cold beverage like fruit juice and sherbets for those hot summer days. There are also hot beverages for rainy days and cold winter days spent indoors. Rose milk and milk shakes with ice cream are ideal for friends coming over for a chat. And for those who want to get experimenting in the kitchen, there's the mocktail option.

Types of Desserts

For me at the end of a meal, a dessert means a sweet dish with chocolate. This is because chocolate does make everything taste better and so is without doubt, my favourite dessert flavouring! But, desserts are also be made with natural fruit flavouring in their season like mango mousse or pineapple upside down cale or a fruit based ice cream like Jamun ice cream, strawberry ice cream etc.

81. Mango Kulfi

Ingredients

5 cups	—	Boiled milk (*Kothikavaitha Paal*)
1 tin	—	Condensed milk (*Sundiya Paal*)
½ cup	—	Sugar (*Sarkarai*)
2 tbsp.	—	Corn flour (*Solla mavu*)
1 cup	—	Mango pulp (*Mam pazhalam kuzhl*)
½ cup	—	Chopped almonds (*Badam parupu*)
½ cup	—	Raisins (*Ularnta thirachai*)

Note: Use any sweet and ripe mango for a good flavour

Method

1. Boil the milk
2. Cool slightly and add sugar
3. Add condensed milk diluted with a little milk
4. Add corn flour
5. Add mango pulp
6. Add Raisins
7. Add blanched and finely chopped almonds
8. Cool completely and only then fill in kulfi moulds. Set in the freezer for 2 hours

9. Remove and remix with a spoon so that the raisins and almonds are uniformly spread throughout the kulfi
10. When half set, insert kulfi sticks in the mould and return to the freezer

Tip: To de-mould the kulfi easily, wet the kulfi mould under running water for a few seconds

82. Hot and Sweet Mango Pickle

Ingredients

4	—	Raw mango (*Mangai*)
½ cup	—	Red chili powder (*Milagai podi*)
½ cup	—	Salt (*Uppu*)
½ cup	—	Sugar (*Sarkarai*)
½ cup + 2 tbsp.	—	Mustard (*Kadugu*)
1 tsp.	—	Fenugreek seeds (*Vendayam*)
1 tsp.	—	Asafoetida (*Perungayam*)
1 cup	—	Gingelly oil (*Nalla ennai*)

Method

1. Wash the mangoes well. Pat dry on a towel. Cut into small cubes with skin. Four mangoes will give 5 cups of mango cubes
2. The ratio for ingredients is Mango cubes 1 : 1/10 salt : 1/10 Sugar: 1/10 Red chili powder
3. In a large glass bowl, add salt to the mango cubes. Cover and keep aside.
4. Everyday, for the next 3 days, stir the salted mango cubes once and cover again
5. On the 4th day, drain the salt water from the salted mango cubes and keep aside
6. Spread out the salted mango cubes on a tray and sun dry
7. In a large wok, dry roast ½ cup of mustard and fenugreek until the mustard splutters and the fenugreek reddens giving a nice aroma
8. Remove from heat and cool completely
9. Grind the roasted mustard, fenugreek in the mixer to a fine powder
10. Add asafoetida and grind again
11. To the salt water drained from the salted mango cubes, add this ground powder, red chili powder and sugar. Mix well with a spoon and make a thick paste
12. In a large wok, heat oil
13. Add 2 tbsp. mustard
14. When the mustard splutters, simmer and add the paste. Mix the paste nicely with the oil
15. Add the mango cubes and mix well to coat every cube with the paste
16. Remove from heat and cool to room temperature. The pickle is ready
17. Fill the pickle in sun dried, sterilized glass bottles when completely cool.

Tip: Never fill bottles with hot pickle. The pickle should be completely cooled before filling into bottles Always store pickles in glass bottles, never in plastic bottles

83. Fish Pickle

Ingredients:

1 kg	–	Seer Fish *(Vanjiram meen)* approx. 7 large pieces, cut into small cubes
7 tbsp.	–	Red chili powder *(Milagai podi)*
1 cup	–	Ginger *(Inji)*, chopped
1 cup	–	Garlic *(Poondu)*
4-1/2 tbsp.	–	Fenugreek seeds *(Vendayam)*
4-1/2 tbsp.	–	Cumin seeds *(Seeragam)*
1-1/2 tbsp.	–	Salt *(Uppu)*
1 tsp.	–	Turmeric powder *(Manjal podi)*
1-1/2 cups	–	Vinegar *(Vinegar)*
1-1/2 cups	–	Gingelly Oil *(Nalla ennai)*
½ cup	–	Tamarind paste *(Puli saaru)*

Method:

1. Wash the fish thoroughly under running water 3 times
2. Wash again with lime to remove any odour
3. Remove all the bones and cut the fish into small cubes
4. Marinate the fish cubes with salt and turmeric
5. Dry the fish in the sun to harden the fish and remove all the moisture
6. Heat oil in a pan and fry the fish cubes till it becomes golden brown

7. Remove the fish cubes and keep aside
8. To make the masala, grind ginger, garlic, fenugreek, cumin and red chili powder together. Do not add any water
9. Add vinegar and grind again
10. In a large wok, heat the same oil used for frying the fish
11. Add the ground masala and mix well
12. Add tamarind paste and mix well
13. Add the fried fish cubes and mix well to coat all the cubes with the masala. The pickle is ready
14. When the pickle thickens, remove from the fire and cool completely
15. Store in sun dried, sterlilized glass bottles

Tip: The same recipe can be used for making prawn pickle.

84. Mango Juice

Ingredients:

1 cup	–	Pulp of Ripe Alphonso Mangoes (Mam pazhalam kuzhl)
2 cups	–	Sugar (Sarkarai)
1 cup	–	Water
1 tbsp.	–	Lime Juice (Elumichai saaru) or citric acid
1/8 tsp.	–	Potassium Meta-bi-Sulphite or K.M.S
¾ tsp.	–	Mango essence
A pinch	–	Orange colour

Method:

1. Wash the mangoes well. Peel the skin and remove the seed
2. Blend the pulp well in a mixer
3. Make sugar syrup by heating water and sugar together over high heat till the sugar dissolves
4. Add citric acid to the sugar syrup and cool completely
5. Add the mango pulp
6. Strain the juice with a strainer
7. Add mango essence and colour and mix well. The mango juice concentrate is ready
8. Dissolve the K.M.S in a little juice and mix well. Now add it to the concentrate. This is the preservative and will keep the mango juice from spoiling for a long time
9. Pour into sun dried, sterilized, glass bottles and preserve in the refrigerator
10. To drink the juice, add 1 part of mango juice concentrate and 3 parts of cold water. Stir well and enjoy the drink

Tip: The same recipe can be used to make grape, orange and pineapple juice also

85. Raw Mango Juice

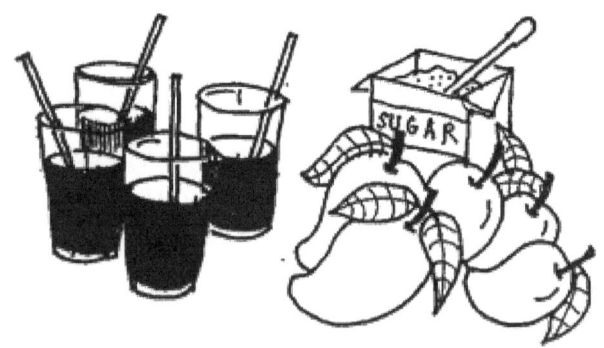

Ingredients:

2	–	Raw Mango, to get 1 cup of Mango pulp *(Mangai kuzhl)*
2 cups	–	Sugar *(Sarkarai)*
1 tsp.	–	Lime Juice *(Elumichai saaru)* or Citric Acid
1/8 tsp.	–	Potassium meta-bi-sulphite or K.M.S
1 cup + ½ cup	–	Water
A pinch	–	Chaat Masala
A few	–	Mint leaves *(Pudina elai)* for garnish

Method:

1. Wash the raw mangoes well. Peel the skin and remove the seed. Chop or grate the mango.
2. Pressure cook the mango with ½ cup of water for 2 whistles to soften the mango
3. Cool and blend in the mixer to get raw mango pulp
4. Prepare sugar syrup by heating 1 cup of water and sugar over high heat till the sugar dissolves
5. Add citric acid to the syrup and cool completely
6. Add the raw mango pulp and mix well
7. Strain using a strainer
8. Dissolve the K.M.S in a little juice and mix well. Now add it to the concentrate. This is the preservative and will keep the raw mango juice from spoiling for a long time. But this juice is best consumed fresh on a hot summer day
9. Pour into sun dried, sterilized, glass bottles and preserve in the refrigerator
10. To drink the juice, add 1 part of mango juice concentrate and 3 parts of cold water.
11. Add a pinch of chaat Masala. Stir well.
12. Garnish with mint leaves and enjoy the drink

Tip: To keep salt flowing freely from a salt cellar, add a few grains of uncooked rice to the salt. This will prevent the salt from becoming sticky

86. Lime Juice

Ingredients:

25	–	Limes to get 2 cups of lime juice (*Elumichai saaru*)
4 cups	–	Sugar (*Sarkarai*)
2 cups	–	Water
A pinch	–	Yellow colour

Method:

1. Wash the limes well and cut into halves
2. Extract the juice from the limes using a lime crusher
3. Make the sugar syrup by heating water and sugar together over high heat till the sugar dissolves
4. Remove from heat and cool completely
5. Add the lime extract and yellow colour. Mix well
6. Strain using a strainer to remove all the seeds. The lime juice concentrate is ready
7. Store in sun dried, sterilized glass bottles and refrigerate
8. To drink the juice, the dilution is 1 part of lime concentrate to 3 parts of cold water. Stir well and enjoy the drink

Tip: To extract maximum juice from a lime, they must be warm. This can be done by microwaving the limes for 20 seconds or rolling them on a hard surface. If limes are cold and taken straight out of the refrigerator, you will get very little juice.

87. Hot and Sweet Lime Pickle

Ingredients:
24	–	Limes (*Elumichai pazham*)
1-1/2 cups	–	Sugar (*Sarkarai*)
1 cup	–	Vinegar
1 cup	–	Red chili powder (*Milagai podi*)
½ cup	–	Salt (*Uppu*)
4 tsp.	–	Cumin seeds (*Seeragam*)
4 tsp.	–	Fenugreek seeds (*Vendayam*)
4 tbsp + 1tbsp	–	Mustard (*Kadugu*)
2 tsp.	–	Asafoetida (*Perungayam*)
1 cup	–	Gingelly oil (*Nalla ennai*)

Method:
1. Wash the limes and dry on a towel in the shade
2. Cut into quarters and remove all the seeds
3. Soak the lime quarters in a glass bowl with sugar, salt and vinegar for 8 days. Every day, stir the lime mixture well once
4. On the ninth day, the lime mixture is ready to be pickled
5. In a wok (kadai) dry roast cumin seeds, fenugreek and 4 tbsp. of mustard. Constantly stir for 2 minutes till the mustard just begins to splutter. Remove from the heat and allow to cool
6. Grind to a fine powder when completely cooled
7. In a large wok, heat oil

8. Add 1tbsp of mustard and chilly powder
9. Add the lime mixture
10. Add the ground powder and mix well
11. Switch off the stove and add asafetida. The pickle is ready
12. Allow the pickle to cool completely before storing in sundried sterilized glass bottles

Tip: To keep limes fresh, place them in a jar of cold water and change the water everyday. Or else rub a little coconut oil on them. But make sure to dry them and make them completely moisture free before making lime pickle

88. Chocolate Ice Cream

Ingredients:

2 tbsp.	–	Cocoa powder (*Cocoa thul*)
1 tbsp.	–	Custard powder (*Cuzhl thul*)
1 cup	–	Boiled milk (*Kothikavaitha Paal*)
½ cup	–	Sugar (*Sarkarai*). Add more to taste
30g	–	Butter (*Vennai*)
½ cup	–	Fresh Cream (*Paal eidu*)
½ cup	–	Raisins (*Ularnta thirachai*) and chopped cashew nuts (*Mundiri*), optional

Method:
1. Heat milk
2. Mix together cocoa and custard powder
3. Add a little warm milk and dissolve the powders in it

4. Add this to the milk when it starts boiling, stirring continuously
5. Add sugar. Check for sweetness and add more if desired
6. Remove from heat and add butter
7. Pour into a bowl and add fresh cream
8. Whisk well and freeze
9. After 1 hour when it is setting, remove from the freezer and whisk again. Reset in freezer
10. After1 hour, remove again and whisk again. Add raisins and nuts if desired. Reset in freezer

Tip: To prevent milk from sticking to the bottom of the milk pan, rinse the pan in water before pouring milk in it

89. Mango Cake

Ingredients:

1 cup	–	Ripe mango pulp (*Mam pazhalam kuzhl*)
1 cup	–	Flour (*Maida mavu*)
1-1/2 cups	–	Powdered sugar (*Poditha sarkarai*)
100g	–	Melted butter (*Vennai*)
2	–	Eggs (*Muttai*)
1 tsp.	–	Baking powder
1 tsp.	–	Mango essence

Method:
1. Sift flour and baking powder three times
2. Separate the eggs and whisk them well

3. Cream butter and sugar
4. Add the well beaten eggs and mix well
5. Add the mango pulp and essence and mix well
6. Beat all the ingredients together to get a smooth batter
7. Fold in the flour and baking powder
8. Pour into a well greased and floured cake tin
9. Bake in a pre-heated oven at 180° for 40 minutes

Tip: Break eggs one by one in separate bowls first. Check if all the eggs are good before mixing them together to be whisked. This way if an egg has gone bad it can be discarded easily.

90. Strawberry Jam & Tri-Colour Sandwich

a) Strawberry Jam

Ingredients:

15	–	Ripe strawberries (Semputru pazhlam)
Equal volume	–	Sugar (Sarkarai), same as strawberry pulp
1 tsp.	–	Raspberry essence
1 tsp.	–	Raspberry colour
A little	–	Sodium benzoate (200 mg: 1 kg pulp)

Method:
1. Cut the strawberries into small pieces and place them in a sauce pan.
2. Add a little water, just enough to cover the fruits

3. Boil till the fruits soften and become tender
4. Strain the cooked fruit to extract the pulp and separate the skin and seeds from it
5. Measure the pulp in a cup. Now, take equal cup measure quantity of sugar (1:1 volume) and mix together
6. Put the pulp and sugar back on the stove. Keep stirring till you get a thick, dropping consistency of jam
7. Add colour and essence
8. Remove from the stove and add sodium benzoate preservative
9. Bottle immediately into dry, sterilized glass bottles and allow to cool and set
10. Only when completely cool, cap the bottles

b) Tri-colour Sandwich

This is a simple but very attractive multi-coloured sandwich. My mother made this often at teatime, for my birthday parties, school picnics and excursions. They were always a hit. The different contrasting hot and sweet tastes when eaten together make it very tasty and unique.

Ingredients:

8	–	Bread slices (*Rotti thundugal*)
1 cup	–	Strawberry jam
½ cup	–	Tomato ketchup (*Thakali sauce*)
1 bunch	–	Coriander leaves (*Kothamali elai*)
4 tbsp.	–	Grated coconut (*Thuruviya thengai*)
1 tsp.	–	Tamarind paste (*Puli*)
1	–	Green chili (*Pachai milagai*)
1	–	Garlic (*Poondu*)
½ tsp.	–	Mustard (*Kadugu*)
½ tsp.	–	Black gram (*Ullutham parupu*)
1 sprig	–	Curry leaves (*Karuvapaellai*), finely chopped
1tbsp. + 1 tbsp.	–	Gingelly oil (*Nalla ennai*)
To taste	–	Salt (*Uppu*) (*Ullutham parupu*)

Method:
1. In a wok, heat 1 tbsp. oil
2. Add green chili
3. Add grated coconut
4. Add garlic and coriander leaves
5. When cool, grind together with tamarind paste and a little hot water
6. Add required salt and grind again to a fine paste
7. In a thalipu chatty, heat oil
8. Add mustard
9. When the mustard splutters, add urad dhal and finely chopped curry leaves
10. Add this to the ground paste and mix well. The coriander chutney is ready
11. To assemble the sandwich, spread butter lightly on the under side of the all the four slices. Start stacking the sandwich from the lowest slice that is spread with coriander chutney. Place a buttered slice on top of it and spread ketchup on it. Place the next buttered slice on top of this and spread strawberry jam on it. Place the last buttered slice on this. The stacking pattern has been shown in the picture below:

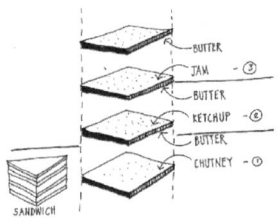

12. First, cut the edges away neatly with a sharp knife. Next cut the stacked sandwich along its' diagonal to get trianglular sandwiches.

Tip: The sun is the best sterilizer. Place the bottles in the mid-day sun for 4–5 hours to completely dry. Any moisture in the bottles will spoil the jam. Sun drying is also the best way to remove any oil or food colouration in glass and plastic containers.

Makeovers with Leftovers

"Give her of the fruit of her hands; and let her own works praise her in the gates"

(Proverbs 31:31)

As a homemaker, I quickly discovered that I hate to waste food. Every attempt was been made in the kitchen to salvage, re-use or recycle left over food. So this section, '**Makeovers with leftovers**' is all about turning little leftovers into a brand-new meal with ease, so good that the second time around they are better than the first. Some are even high yielding and remunerative like **Ghee**. Through my recipes in this section, I have attempted to answer a few questions that you may have.

Question 1: What could I do with over-ripe bananas other than a cosmetic facemask?

Making **Banana cake** is probably the best way to use over ripe bananas that can only be thrown out. The riper the bananas, the tastier the cake! However, this cake has a short shelf life and must be consumed within a day or two, as it tends to spoil otherwise. **Banana paniyaram** is another way to use over-ripe bananas and is one of the tastiest snack recipes for an evening snack.

Question 2: What could I do with stale bread or left over bread?

The best way to use left over bread is to sundry it and make it into **Rusk** for crust coating cutlets, fried prawns and fish etc., Stale bread can be made into **Bread pudding**. This pudding tastes better the next day when eaten cold.

Question 3: What could I do with one piece of chicken or meat leftover?

Pizza is the sure answer. This is the best makeover recipe for 2 or 3 leftover pieces of chicken in a curry. The only effort required is to stock up a few pizza bases from a bakery.

Question 4: What could I do with milk that has curdled accidently or too much milk remaining before a long journey?

Curdled milk or over-stocked milk need not be thrown away but can be used to make delicious rasogollas or paneer. *But never ever used spoiled milk as it causes food poisoning.*

Get creative with leftovers and you'll be a makeover Goddess soon!

91. Banana Cake

Ingredients:

2	–	Over ripe bananas (*Vazhai pazham*), mashed
2 cups	–	Flour (*Maida mavu*)
1	–	Eggs (*Muttai*)
100 g	–	Butter (*Vennai*)
1 cup	–	Powdered sugar (*Poditha sarkarai*)
1/2 tsp.	–	Baking soda (*Aapa soda*)
2 tsp.	–	Baking powder
1 tsp.	–	Vanilla essence (*Vanilla saarai*)
3 tbsp.	–	Curds (*Thayir*)
½ cup	–	Chopped cashewnuts (*Mundiri*)

Method:

1. Cream melted butter and sugar well
2. Add egg beaten well with vanilla essence. Whisk well
3. Add mashed bananas
4. Sift the flour with baking soda and baking powder
5. Fold in the flour mixture
6. Add curds
7. Pour out the batter into a well greased and floured baking tray
8. Sprinkle chopped nuts dusted in a little flour
9. Bake in a preheated oven at 180' for 45 minutes

Tip: Do not discard butter wrappers. They are ideal for greasing cake tins and cookie trays before the batter is poured in.

92. Bread Pudding

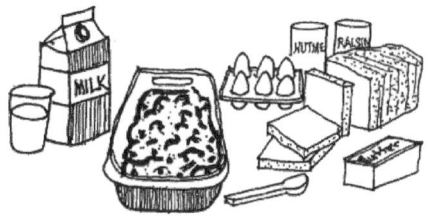

Ingredients:

6	–	Bread slices (*Roti thundugal*), edges removed and torn into crumbs
2 cups	–	Boiled milk (*Kothikavaitha Paal*)
50 g	–	Butter (*Vennai*)
2/3 cup	–	Sugar (*Sarkarai*)
3	–	Eggs (*Muttai*)
2 tsp.	–	Cinnamon powder (*Ilavankappattai thul*)
½ tsp.	–	Ground nutmeg (*Jathikai thul*), optional
1 tsp.	–	Vanilla essence (*Vanilla saarai*)
½ cup	–	Raisins (*Ularnta thirachai*)

Method:

1. Boil the milk
2. Add butter to the milk and stir well
3. Remove from the stove and cool till lukewarm
4. Beat together eggs, sugar, powdered cinnamon, nutmeg and vanilla essence in a mixer for a minute
5. Add buttered milk to the batter
6. Place the bread crumbs in a greased baking tray
7. Sprinkle raisins here and there
8. Pour the batter over the bread

9. Bake the pudding in a pre-heated oven at 170' for 45 minutes

Tip: Do not discard the two end slices of a bread loaf. They are ideal for making homemade breadcrumbs for cutlets. Crumble these bread slices and sun dry in the hot sun or else dry roast in a hot tava. Grind finely in the mixer to get breadcrumbs. Store in an airtight container

93. Kothu Parotta

Ingredients:

1	–	Left over parotta
2 or 3	–	Left over chicken pieces
½ cup	–	Left over chicken gravy *(thick)*
2	–	Eggs *(Muttai)*
1	–	Onions *(Vengayam)*, julienned
1	–	Tomatoes *(Thakali)*, julienned
1	–	Green chilies *(Pachai milagai)*, finely chopped
1 sprig	–	Curry leaves *(Karuvapaellai)*
1 tsp.	–	Cumin seeds *(Seeragam)*
½ cup	–	Coriander leaves *(Kothamali elai)*, finely chopped
½ tsp.	–	Turmeric powder *(Manjal podi)*
1 tsp.	–	Coriander powder *(Malli podi)*
½ tsp.	–	Red chili powder *(Milagai podi)*
3 tbsp.	–	Gingelly oil *(Nalla ennai)*

Method:
1. Heat oil in a large wok
2. Season with cumin seeds
3. Add finely chopped onion and curry leaves
4. When the onions slightly brown add the tomatoes finely chopped
5. Add the egg and scramble it in the onion and tomato mix
6. Add the shredded chicken pieces and check for salt. If needed add salt
7. Add turmeric powder, chili powder and coriander powder (This step can be omitted if sufficient chicken gravy is there)
8. Add the chopped parotta pieces and toss well
9. Add the chicken gravy and mix everything together so that the gravy coats every piece of the parotta
10. Turn the heat to simmer and cover the wok. Let it cook for about 2 minutes
11. Remove the lid and add finely chopped coriander leaves
12. Serve hot with onion raita and chicken gravy

Tip: Same recipe can be used with left over idiyappam instead of parotta

94. Aloo Paratta

Ingredients:

1 cup	–	Left over potato poriyal (*Recipe 64*)
2 cups	–	Wheat Flour (*Gothumai mavu*)
To taste	–	Salt (*Uppu*)
As required	–	Water
1 tbsp.	–	Gingelly oil (*Nalla ennai*)
½ cup	–	Ghee (*Nei*) for cooking

Method:

1. In a deep bowl, knead together sifted wheat flour, salt and left over potato poriyal
2. Add water as required and knead well
3. Add oil and knead well
4. Make large balls and flatten slightly.
5. Dust in wheat flour and roll out the parattas on a floured board
6. Place each paratta on a hot tava and cook on both sides
7. Smear with ghee

Tip: Place a tea towel in a large casserole. Keep all the aloo parattas piled up and wrapped together in the tea towel. Cover with a lid. This will ensure that the parattas stay soft for a long time.

95. Pizza

Ingredients:

2 or 3	–	Left over chicken pieces from chicken curry
2	–	Ready-made Pizza base
1	–	Onions (**Vengayam**), finely chopped
1	–	Tomatoes (**Thakali**), finely chopped
1/2	–	Green capsicum (**Kudai milagai**), finely chopped
¼ tsp.	–	Turmeric powder (**Manjal podi**)
1 tsp.	–	Coriander powder (**Malli podi**)

½ tsp.	–	Red chili powder (*Milagai podi*)
2 tbsp.	–	Pizza sauce
5	–	Olives (*Olive*), cut into halves
½ cup	–	Mozarella cheese (*Thuruviya mozzarella cheese*), grated
½ cup	–	Coriander leaves (*Kothamali elai*)
1 tsp.	–	Oregano or carom (*Omam*)
2 tbsp.	–	Tomato ketchup (*Thakali sauce*)
2 tbsp.	–	Gingelly oil (*Nalla ennai*)

Method:
1. Shred the chicken
2. In a wok, heat 2 tbsp. oil
3. Add onions and saute till they turn transparent
4. Add capsicum
5. When the onions turn transparent, toss in the shredded chicken
6. Add turmeric, coriander, red chili powder and salt. Mix well
7. Add tomatoes
8. Simmer and cook under a closed lid for 2 minutes
9. Remove from heat
10. On a greased pizza tray, set the pizza
11. Spread pizza sauce on the pizza
12. Add the chicken as topping
13. Sprinkle olives on top
14. Grate mozzarella cheese on top
15. Bake in a pre-heated oven at 250°C for 8 minutes
16. While serving, sprinkle oregano, chilly flakes and drizzle tomato ketchup on top. Serve hot

Tip: Before grating cheese, apply some oil in the grater to prevent it from sticking. Also, spray the cup with oil before measuring honey so that it comes out fully without sticking.

96. Bread Gulab Jamun

Ingredients:

2 cups	–	Left over sugar syrup from Gulab Jamun (*Sarkarai paku*)
8 slices	–	Left over bread (*Roti thundugal*)
½ cup	–	Boiled milk (*Kothikavaitha Paal*)
5	–	Almonds, blanched (*Badam parupu*)
3 cups	–	Refined sunflower oil for frying (*Poripathuku ennai*)
2 tbsp.	–	Ghee (*Nei*)

Method:

1. Remove the crust from the bread edges
2. Add milk and knead into a soft dough
3. Make small balls
4. Put an almond piece in the centre and re-roll
5. Heat oil for frying. Add ghee
6. Fry the bread balls in the oil till golden brown
7. Dip the fried balls in the sugar syrup

Tip: To peel the skin of almonds, tomatoes or peaches, simply soak them in boiling water for 5–10 minutes. The skin can be easily removed

97. Rasogollas

Ingredients:
4 cups	–	Curdled Milk after boiling
1 tsp.	–	Flour (*Maida mavu*)
1 tsp.	–	Baking powder
1-1/2 cups	–	Sugar (*Sarkarai*)
5 cups	–	Water

Method:
1. Cool the curdled milk and strain to separate the curd cheese from the whey water
2. Remove the thickened curd cheese and tie it in a muslin cloth. Hang the muslin cloth for 2 hours over a bowl for all the excess water to drain. Wash the curd cheese under running cold water to remove sourness, if any
3. Add flour and baking powder. Knead well. At first it will not bind but continuous kneading will bind it well. This is the secret of firm and good rasogollas
4. Make small balls, as they will swell to double their size when cooked
5. Boil water and sugar in a large pot or pressure cooker
6. After five minutes when the sugar has dissolved, drop the rasogolla balls slowly and carefully into the sugar syrup, one by one
7. Cover and cook for 15 minutes
8. Remove the lid and cook for 10 minutes

Tip: Rasogollas taste best when stored and served in a mud pot

98. Banana Paniyaram

Ingredients:

2	–	Over ripe bananas (*Vazhai pazham*)
1 cup	–	Flour (*Maida mavu*)
1	–	Eggs (*Muttai*)
½ tsp.	–	Baking soda (*Aapa soda*)
½ tsp.	–	Vanilla essence (*Vanilla saarai*)
½ cup	–	Boiled milk (*Kothikavaitha Paal*)
3 cups	–	Refined sunflower oil for frying (*Poripathuku ennai*)

Method:

1. Mash the bananas
2. Add all the other ingredients and blend in the mixer to get a smooth batter of dropping consistency. Add more milk if necessary
3. Heat a little oil in a kuzhi paniyaram chatti (or you can deep fry in hot oil)
4. Drop spoonsful of the batter carefully into the hot oil. Simmer
5. When the lower side has cooked and browned, turn over and cook the other side also. Serve hot or cold

Tip: Sieves, sifters and graters can be cleaned thoroughly with a toothbrush dipped in soapy water. Rinse and dry before putting away to be stored.

99. Rice Kheer

Ingredients:

1 cup	–	Left over cooked rice, preferably basmati rice, (*Basmati arisi*)
1-1/2 cups	–	Boiled milk (*Kothikavaitha Paal*)
2 tbps	–	Ghee (*Nei*)
2 tbsp.	–	Chopped cashewnuts (*Mundiri*)
2 tbsp.	–	Raisins (*Ularnta thirachai*)
10 tbsp.	–	Sugar (*Sarkarai*)
½ tsp.	–	Cardamom powder (*Elakai podi*)
½ tin	–	Condensed milk (*Sundiya Paal*)

Method:

1. Heat ghee in a pan
2. Fry cashewnuts in it
3. Add raisins next and fry lightly. Keep aside
4. In a sauce pan heat the milk
5. Add rice slightly mashed
6. Add sugar
7. Add powdered cardamom
8. Add condensed milk diluted with a little milk
9. Add fried cashewnuts and raisins
10. Mix well. Serve hot or cold

Tip: Puddings, Kheer or Phirni that contain milk should never be cooked in aluminium vessels as it imparts a slight colour to any milk product cooked in them for a long time

100. Ghee

Ingredients:
2 cups — Fresh cream (*Paal eidu*), collected from boiled milk everyday

Method:
1. Collect the cream that settles on top of milk after it is boiled and cooled. This is **Fresh Cream**
2. When milk is set for curds, add the fresh cream
3. The next day when curd is set, a thick layer of **Butter Cream** will form at the top
4. Collect the butter cream in a separate vessel everyday for a week
5. At the end of the week a substantial amount of butter cream will collect. Beat this well in the mixer
6. A thick, frothy mixture will first form
7. Add a cup of ice cold water and continue to beat in the mixer
8. After a while, lumps of yellow **Butter** will separate from the buttermilk
9. In a large wok, collect all the butter and melt over high heat on the stove. Let it bubble and froth
10. After a while, the bubbling will stop and a golden transparent liquid will form. This is **Ghee**. Strain and store in a sterilized container.

Tip: If you find that you need more ghee or oil in the pan while sautéing, add it in a stream along the edges of the pan. This way by the time the ghee/oil reaches the ingredient being sautéed, it will be heated

Appendix

1. Setting up your Kitchen

Nothing is more exciting than setting up your very own kitchen. As a child, I had my dollhouse kitchen where my friends and I would fashion out mud cakes and mud coffee and serve them in play teacups and saucers! As I look back, I remember that was so much fun. So the transition from play time to the real thing was really exciting.

To go shopping for your kitchen and contemplating buying everything on display or in the brochure is certainly tempting. But budget planning and buying only what is absolutely essential is a good idea at the beginning. In this section, I have suggested kitchenware, tools and applicances that I have in my kitchen and would advise you to also own. I would advise not buying all at once but collecting one by one over the years to celebrate an anniversary, a birthday or just a memorable vacation. You can aquire a few essentials like a branded pressure cooker, a pot, pan, wok and a few kitchen tools and then collect slowly.

My personal favourite material for cookware, storage containers and cutlery is Stainless steel and hence I call my kitchen, *An Eversilver Kitchen*. I have disposed off all plastics and multi-coloured kitchenware and have started collecting only stainless steel cookware. Gradually, my kitchen has transformed into a black and eversilver theme kitchen. Even applicances like the refrigerator, kettle and microwave oven in my kitchen are eversilver and black. Eversilver has its own advantages and disadvantages. It's longlasting, easy to clean and unbreakable thus making it the perfect material for cookware. Its shiny appearance adds cosmetic charm to the kitchen and dining table. Containers do not stain easily and are leak proof, hence you can use it for storing most condiments and grains. The only disadvantage is that however superior the quality of the stainless steel, it still cannot withstand eroding by salt. Hence salt and salted items like pickle cannot be stored in stainless steel containers.

Whatever your taste is, choose a colour theme or concept for your kitchen while purchasing cookware. Always choose carefully, quality over quantity and low pricing.

2. Electrical Applicances

A gas stove and lighter are the first buy for a kitchen but you can also go for something more multi-functional like a cooking range with cooking, grilling and baking functions. Other than the stove, the absolute necessary applicances a kitchen must have are a refrigerator and a mixer. All other gadgets or "kitchen toys" can be collected over time.

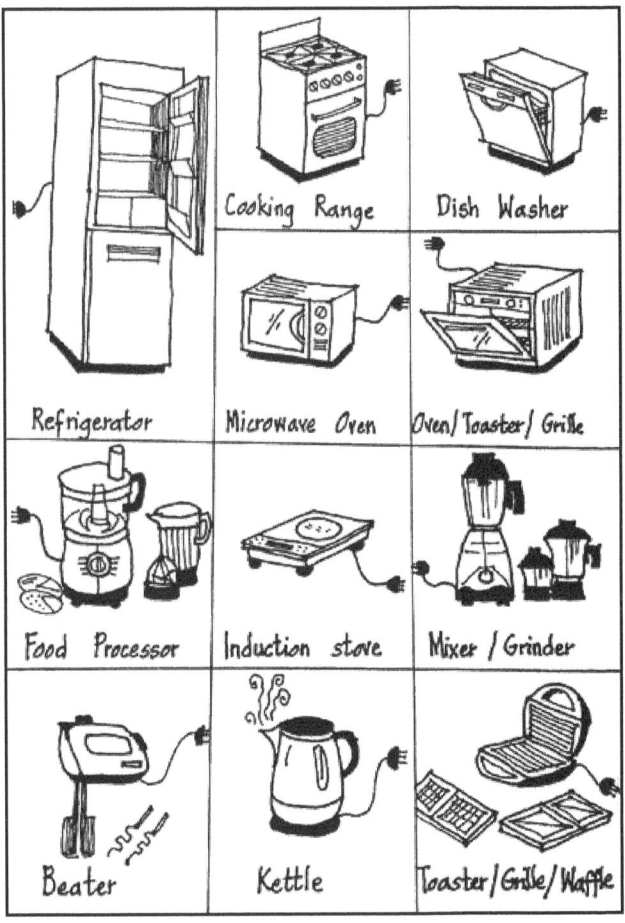

3. Cooking Utensils

A shallow wok can be used for sauteing vegetables or for making scrambled eggs and noodles whereas a deep pot can be used to make curries and gravies. Do remember to have separate flat pans for making dosais, omelettes and chapatis. Also, do keep separate cookware for sweets and savouries, vegetarian and non-vegetarian dishes.

Some breakfast dishes need special cookware to make them like the Puttu maker, Kuzhi paniyaram pan and Appam pan. But some cookware can be used for making other dishes. The idly steamer can be used for steaming dishes other than idlies, like iddiyappam, kozhukattai etc., A double boiler for milk, a seasoning pan and a press for making muruku, om podi etc., ate good purchases for the kitchen.

4. Kitchen Tools

I love collecting kitchen tools! It's like a hobby by itself. There are many tools for different food preparation and they do help to make cooking easier and effortless. I have listed a few tools that I have in my kitchen.

- Tongs for gripping hot vessels, turning and flipping food like salads
- Ladles for serving gravies, curries and soups
- Whisks for whisking cream, eggs and batter. They are the best tools for beating batter and removing lumps.
- A rolling pin for rolling out dough for pastries and chapatis

- Spatulas help to flip omelettes, dosais and pancakes
- Spoons are ideal for serving and stirring food
- An Egg separator is a helpful tool when the recipe calls for egg whites separated from yolks like making mousse etc.,
- A Masher is used to mash potatoes

- A Gnocchi board for making rolled snacks or pasta
- A Grater is a must-have for grating cheese, carrots, beetroot and other vegetables for making salads and poriyals
- Pitters and Corers for removing seeds in fruits etc.,

5. Storage Containers

Food storage containers help to keep your kitchen and pantry organized and in top shape while maintaining the shelf life of the food stored in them. They must be airtight and sealed well to keep food stuff stored in them fresh while preserving natural flavours, preventing insects and extending shelf life.

1. Essentials   -   Rice, Wheat, Sugar
2. Lentils   -   Dhals, Maida, Besan, Snacks etc.
3. Masalas   -   Powders, Tea, Coffee etc.
4. Condiments & Spices   -   Anjarey Petti

Salt and salt containing foods like pickles must be stored in glass bottes and never in eversilver containers. So, while purchasing containers, care must be taken to select the rght type of container considering factors like type of storage (open or refrigerated), length of storage (perishable or non-perishable) and storage space (large for essential grains, medium for lentils and small for masalas).

6. The Spice Box

In a traditional South Indian kitchen the spice box is called '*Anj-arey petti*' meaning, '*A box with five and a half compartments*'. Of course today, with the easy availability of readily ground masalas and spices in the market, this spice box is no longer a five but rather a seven-compartment box with tiny spoons in each compartment. In my kitchen, I call it, '*The jewel box*'! because of the beautiful colours of the masalas and their stunning flavours. I would recommend purchasing a spice box to every new bride as it is a very practical must-have in every kitchen. Here's why!

Indian dishes use many different kinds of spices and seeds that are either dry roasted or lightly fried in oil and then ground into powder or paste form for curries and gravies. They are used for seasoning the oil in the case of vegetable stir-fries. Hence it is absolutely essential to have all of them in one collective box at an easy-to-reach point near the cooking stove. This will eliminate running after and reaching into ten or twenty large storage tins to pick out spices when the oil is hot and ready to be seasoned. The spice box contains spices and ground masalas in 50g–100g quantities depending on the size of the compartments. These tempering ingredients and masalas are added in only tablespoon or teaspoon measures while cooking, but they are really the ones that add aromatic flavours, heat and colour to a dish.

It's really a matter of personal taste and choice but I would advise you to have 3 such boxes:

1. For storing ground masalas like Sambar powder, turmeric powder, coriander powder, pepper ppwder, garam masala
2. For storing Indian tempering spices like Mustard, Cumin seeds, Black gram, Bengal gram etc.,

3. For storing Western spices like Rosemary, Thyme, Oregano

There are many types available in the market like plastic, metal and wooden spice boxes. Choose the one you like. Here's a tip – Do remember to keep the spice box tightly closed when not in use to preserve all the precious flavours.

7. Prep Tools In The Kitchen

Prep tools like a Mortar and Pestle are those that help you to prep food before they are cooked. A good quality cutting board and set of knives will help you chop, dice and cut at ease and last a long time.

8. Kitchen Fashion

9. Entertaining in your Home

Once you have set up your home, you can start inviting friends and family over for a meal, a party or get-to-gether. I have given you a few guidelines for entertaining with two table settings, formal – Continental and traditional – South Indian, to get you started.

a) Continental Table Setting

The continental style is thought of as a more stylish, formal and graceful way of eating. There are protocols and the "proper" way to eat food. Food is eaten with a 'cut and consume' technique with the aid of a fork, knife and spoon. It is never hand eaten. The consumption of the meal is silent. As shown in the drawings, the guest gestures non-verbally by positioning his fork and knife in different ways to indicate in-between bites, his appreciation or disapproval of the meal etc.,

In a continental table setting, knowing how to use your fork, spoon and knife is an important part of table etiquette. Setting the table itself is an art for the host. But the guest also plays his part during and after the meal. At the start of the meal, the napkin that is placed on the left of the plate is neatly unfolded and spread on the lap by the guest. The meal is three courses with starters and appetisers followed by the main course and finished off with dessert. They are all served separately, one after the other.

There are separate bowls and plates for every dish like salad plate, cereal bowl, soup bowl etc. The sizes of the plates vary with the dish like the main dinner plate in the centre and the small bread plate on the side. There are also different forks, spoons and knives for every dish and for eating fish, salads and meat. The knife is always held in the left hand. Depending on the meal, the spoon or knife are held in the right hand. At the end of the meal, the guest leaves his napknin unfolded to the right of the plate indicating, "He is finished".

Table Setting

Table setting:

Breakfast	Lunch	Dinner
1. Napkin	1. Napkin	1. Napkin
2. Plate	2. Plate	2. Plate
3. Fork	3. Fork	3. Dinner fork
4. Knife	4. Knife	4. Dinner knife
5. Water glass	5. Water glass	5. Water glass
6. Table napkin	6. Table napkin	6. Table napkin
7. Butter knife	7. Dessertspoon	7. Butter knife
8. Bread plate	8. Salad fork	8. Bread plate
9. Juice	9. Coffee cup	9. Wine glass
10. Coffee cup	10. Soup bowl	10. Salad plate
11. Sugar spoon	11. Soupspoon	11. Dessertspoon
12. Cereal spoon	12. Butter knife	12. Salad fork
	13. Bread dish	13. Teaspoon
		14. Soup spoon

b) South Indian Meal Setting

A typical South Indian meal is served on a banana leaf and is eaten by hand only. The "*Elai Sapadu*" is wholesome, festive, unapologetically traditional and an experience.

The banana leaf is always kept folded towards the inside until the guest is seated and ready for the meal. Once seated, the guest lightly washes the leaf with a sprinkling of water. The meal is then served on a wet banana leaf, all at once.

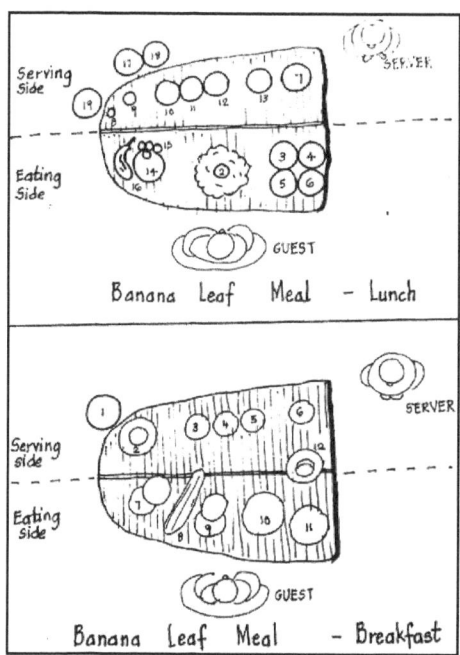

In a breakfast meal, the starter is a semi-solid sweet like kesari or sweet pongal. Breakfast consists of a variety of "*tiffin*" items like idly, dosai, poori, oothapam, ven pongal etc., and these are placed on the lower or eating side of the banana leaf. The side dishes like curries and chutneys are placed on the upper or serving side. The meal is finished off with vadai and hot coffee. Water is always kept at the top left corner of the leaf.

In a lunch or dinner meal also, the starter is a solid sweet like ladoo or halwa. Rice is the nucleus and the central dish on the leaf. It is eaten as a three-course meal with sambar, then rasam and lastly with curd. All the other dishes compliment the rice like the poriyal, applam, pickle etc., The meal is nicely finished off with a liquid sweet dish like payasam or kheer and a banana.

When the meal is over, the guest folds the leaf inwards as it was before as sign of respect, goodwill and an implication that the guest enjoyed the meal. Folding the leaf away from you is taken as a sign of disrespect, illwill and implies that the guest did not enjoy the meal. In complete contrast to a silent consumption of the meal in continental dining and as bizzare as it may sound, slurping and licking of the fingers is not considered uncouth by the host, but rather as a sign of enjoyment of the meal by the guest!

Arrangement of Dishes

Breakfast

1. Water
2. Coffee
3. Coconut chutney
4. Tomato chutney
5. Coriander chutney
6. Kesari/ Sweet
7. Idly
8. Dosai
9. Poori
10. Pongal
11. Sambar
12. Vadai

Lunch/Dinner

1. Rice
2. Ghee
3. Dhal
4. Rasam
5. Sambar
6. Kara kozhambu
7. Curd
8. Salt
9. Pickle
10. Avial
11. Poriyal
12. Kootu
13. Sweet
14. Applam
15. Chips
16. Banana
17. Paal payasam
18. Parupu payasam
19. Water

10. Writing your Recipe Journal

Ingredients for Success

There are thousands of recipe books in the bookstore and perhaps you have cookbooks galore in your bookshelf at home. But, writing down recipes and keeping your very own recipe book is like a kitchen journal or a diary; a treasure trove of experience, history and love, all rolled into one book.

I have already confessed to being a "taught" cook who learnt to cook. During the early days, cooking seemed like a cumbersome and hard chore. That's when I started writing down recipes like a reference book or a kitchen encyclopedia. To make my endeavour more interesting to me, I decided to personalise my recipe collection, besides the number of assorted recipe books that I purchased from a bookstore. I bought A5 size good quality white paper and had them well bound into several 250-paged rexin bound books. I remember the day they arrived from the binder's shop. They looked so good that I started writing down a recipe on the very first day!

A Typical Page in My Recipe Book has the Following

1. **Title** or name of the dish. Below it is written the type of dish in brackets like *Appetiser*, *Entrée* or *Dessert* and the type of cuisine like *Chinese, Mexican, South Indian, Konkan* etc.,

2. **Source** of the recipe i.e whom or where I learnt the recipe from, as I collected recipes from everywhere and from everybody – aunts, neighbours, friends, cousins, the Internet, cooking shows on TV, newspapers, cooking magazines and even the back of tin wrappers. Some recipes I learnt on a holiday weekend at a cousin's place, others at cooking classes, baking retreats and at the women's fellowship in our church.
3. **List of Ingredients** and their measures (*British* weight measures or *American* cup measures)
4. **Method of preparation** in steps of 1, 2, 3.... I also added the vessel to be used for cooking or baking like **wok, pot, saucepan**, kind of serving and garnishing for the dish.
5. **Tips and Notes.** Whenever I tried a recipe in the kitchen, I updated my recipe book with a post-it of do's and don't's. I also added a footnote of who loved the dish when I made it and whose favourite it had become in the family.
6. **Sketch or picture** of the dish. I bought second hand cooking magazines to widen my horizon of recipes and neatly cut out the recipes that I liked and pasted them in my book with a good quality adhesive to avoid staining the pages. Every week the Sunday special newspaper had a special cooking edition with photograhs so this added colour to my book. Whenever a picture was not available, I resorted to hand sketching especially special folding techniques, icing procedures, garnishing etc.,

Dear new bride, I encourage you to definitely start writing your own recipe book, something personal and very close to the heart. Not just for you but it can be a gift for someone dear. In my case, someday I hope to pass on my collection of hand-written recipe books to my daughter and granddaughter as "Grandma's Cookbooks". But you can get together as cousins or friends and gift a collective handwritten themed cookbook for a bridal or baby shower. Or you can write out some of your niece's favourite recipes and gift it to her on her 16th birthday or her wedding day as a gift. Or gift a handwritten cookbook of baking recipes to your child's favourite teacher as a 'Thankyou' gesture. Whatever the occasion a personalized recipe book is sure to be a hit!

About the Author

Satya Sudhir is a professor of Architecture and has published several award winning research papers in the field of Architecture. But, her inspiration to venture into non-technical writing was triggered when she won the creative writing contest at I.I.T. Madras in 2000. Since then, she has been writing for newspapers and magazines on everyday subjects. '*A hundred red roses – A cookbook for the new bride*' is a collection of recipes from her kitchen and has been written exclusively for a new bride who wants to learn cooking. This is her first book.

Her other interests include art and singing gospel music.

Dear bride,

I would love to hear from you! If you loved my (book) bouquet of, '*A hundred red roses*', do write in to me at: hemera@rediffmail.com

– Satya Sudhir

Author & Illustrations Designer: Dr. Satya Sudhir
203, Sims Manor, 3rd 'A' Main, 1st stage, 2nd Block, H.B.R Layout, Bangalore – 560 043.
E-mail: hemera@rediffmail.com